TEN THOUSAND SHELLS AND COUNTING: A MEMOIR

BOOK 1 IN THE TEENAGE WAR SURVIVAL SERIES

NADIJA MUJAGIC

PIONEER PUBLISHING

To my beloved parents, Munib and Azra.
My heroes.

FOREWORD

"Dr. Wexler... Dr. Wexler, wake up!"

My psychotherapist was a gentleman in his eighties who, remarkably, had never written notes during our sessions, but memorized almost every detail I had shared with him over several years. As my workplace was around the corner from his office, I'd visit him during my lunch break once a week. More often than not, I'd see him walking around Cambridge, his tall figure bent on one side. He was legally blind, so I never attempted to say hello, thinking he'd never see and recognize me. He fell asleep in his chair often, and I would yell out his name until he was alert again.

"Dr. Wexler, why do you fall asleep during the session? This is not what I'm paying you for."

"I can't help it. There's something you're not telling me, so I doze off involuntarily."

After several months of seeing Dr. Wexler on a weekly basis, he gave me an official diagnosis—PTSD or post-traumatic stress disorder. When I came home and looked up on the Internet what that exactly meant, it came as no surprise. According to the National Institutes of Health website, a person suffering from PTSD may re-experience traumatic events through flashbacks, bad dreams, or frightening thoughts. The person may feel emotionally numb, depressed, or may experience strong guilt for extended periods of time.

When I turned fourteen, a war broke out in my country, Yugoslavia, back then, and now Bosnia and Herzegovina. Ever since the war ended, I have had two recurring dreams. In one dream, a war was about to start again, and I planned to commit suicide or escape, because, recollecting my neighbors' experience, I would be too afraid to face people who would have my life in their hands and dispose or do whatever they please with it. In another dream, the same enemy occupied a neighborhood my family and I lived in, and we were all in hiding, waiting to be found and executed on the spot. These dreams were often vivid, and they would wake me up just as a shell blasted or the enemy got closer in my dream. These dreams were as horrifying and real as the experience once was.

In recounting both the dreams and war stories in my head, I have felt desperately alone, as though no soul could ever sympathize or understand who I was and what caused me to with-draw or become distant from even myself. Yet, going through this experience, I know I am not alone. As I write this, there are wars going on in several countries. No matter what country a war takes place in, I'm almost certain that the story I'm about to tell is like many of those stories by victims of these terrible events.

When I first came to the United States, I found a temporary job at Harvard University, scheduling audio visual equipment for classes and studying sessions. My shared desk was in the basement of the Science Center, which has never seen a ray of sunshine. It was dark and depressing, and if you were claustrophobic, you would probably need to quit on your second day of the job. One day, I noticed my colleague's speech, his lisp getting on my nerves, and it felt as if a thousand little bugs were crawling on my skin and I was trying to escape. When he whistled, I would cringe, and my body would become so tense that I wanted to run as fast as I could.

Many years later, I discovered that the disease is called misophonia, or, as literal translation would suggest, "a hatred for sounds." As the disease progressed, I had noticed many other sounds driving me insane. When I attempted to get help from a professional, the disease was not well studied to date and that there was no known cure. But there could be methods developed to minimize the impact of the inconveniences so that your daily life was normalized and you didn't have to run away from many social situations and interactions. For example, meditation would help. The therapist told me that my central nervous system was most likely damaged, which made my senses much more sensitive than those of an average person. In recollecting all my war experiences, that certainly made sense. During the three-and-half-year war, I must have heard over ten thousand shells falling near me, causing me to twitch, jump, and react in terror and fear. Ten thousand shells seemed like a drop in the ocean, a tiny piece of scab on an old wound.

In his attempt to help me deal with PTSD, Dr. Wexler listened with kindness and non-judgment. When I felt depressed and anxious, he would tell me that prescription drugs were not the way to go. Instead, he would tell me, "You need to talk, Nadija. Get all this out of your system."

So here I am. Timely or not, I have made a conscious decision to tell my war story. This is the story of a girl who spent most of her teenage years in a war. These are the events that led up to the person I am today. As I write this memoir, I think of all past, present, and future PTSD victims, whether their PTSD was caused by a state of an armed conflict between different nations or simply by an internal struggle. Regardless of what causes traumatic events, I know they breed pain.

Remember to be gentle and kind to yourself.

CHAPTER 1

⚜

The Beginnings

*T*he military don't start wars. Politicians start wars.
—William Westmoreland

"WE WILL NO LONGER BE in control if we get into a situation where Croatia and Slovenia were, especially Croatia. That hell would be a thousand times worse in Bosnia and Herzegovina. There would be no way to stop it. I ask you once again, I am not threatening, I am pleading...that you take seriously the political will of the Serbian people represented here by the Serbian Democratic Party, the Serbian Renewal Movement and some Serbs from other parties. I plead with you to fully understand that what you are doing is not good. The road that you are choosing for Bosnia and Herzegovina is the same highway to hell and suffering that Slovenia and Croatia have already taken. Do not think that you will not take Bosnia and Herzegovina to hell and the Muslim people maybe into extinction."

"You son of a bitch!" my father yelled at the TV screen as Radovan Karadžić calmly stood at the podium talking into a microphone, with his wild white hair and a pronounced chin dimple.

"Quiet, Munib. The neighbors will hear you," my mother whispered, timid.

"I don't care! I would punch this son of a bitch right now if I could!"

My father was not a violent man. In fact, he was sweet, always smiling and friendly to the neighbors and their kids. He was born right after World War II in a family of four other siblings, with parents, like most people, struggling to provide for their children in the war aftermath. Growing up, my father had no shoes to wear, so before he went to school, he had to wait for his older brother to return home so he could wear his pair. My grandfather, from the stories I had heard, was violent, quick to lose temper and take it out on my grandmother. My grandmother, a quiet and sweet lady, always smiled when we came to visit. She had beautiful bright blue eyes, with one eye sparkling in the right light. My father told us one day that my grandfather punched my grandmother's eye, causing her to lose it and have it replaced with a fake one. My father didn't get along with his father, and he strived not to become like him. As much as he resisted resembling his father, he couldn't help it. When sporadic bickering with my mother ensued, they yelled and screamed at each other. But the children—my older sister, Amra, and I—would observe and eventually got used to their form of communication. We knew they wouldn't lay their hand on us.

As my father Munib listened to Karadžić, he was growing red, angry, unable to control his composure. Karadžić's threat was uncalled for. His calm deliverance of potential chaos to come seemed provoking, arrogant, something to cope with in the only way one could—angrily. I had not seen my father this angry ever since Amra disobeyed my parents and not come home until a couple of hours after her curfew. My parents were strict. When she arrived home around midnight, for the first and only time I had witnessed, my father took a belt out and beat the crap out of her. She cried, and I cried with her to ease the pain.

In October 1991, the war in Croatia was in full swing. Karadžić was giving a speech in the Bosnian Parliament in response to Bosnia's mandate to separate from Yugoslavia. I didn't know what it all meant, this whole business with Croatia, and now Bosnia. There was war there, there could be war here, but I couldn't even picture what that might look like. The only thing I could think of were my maternal grandmother's words when we, her grandchildren, had left food crumbs on the table: "Eat up everything. God forbid if war broke out. You would have nothing to eat." She had survived World War I and II. I did not know what war looked like outside of old World War II footage I had watched on TV when I was sick and bundled in blankets, excused from school. Like the footage suggested, I imagined a bunch of soldiers getting out of the trench and running as fast as possible toward the enemy line while pointing the gun in the enemy's direction. Above would be a flock of planes dropping bombs on the land while soldiers were falling and dying in their distinct hard olive helmets and uniforms. Civilians would stay home and watch plane parades from the windows, and when needed, they would run to the shelter to hide from the attack. My grandmother never shared her war stories, and no one ever asked. Perhaps she was just old and had to say these things to show off her wisdom of age.

Karadžić's speech continued. As he uttered the words of urgent threat, chills went down my spine.

"Because if a war breaks out, the Muslim people will not be able to defend themselves."

CHAPTER 2

❦

Home

War may sometimes be a necessary evil. But no matter how necessary, it is always an evil, never a good. We will not learn how to live together in peace by killing each other's children.
—Jimmy Carter

MY PARENTS, Amra, and I lived in a suburb of Sarajevo, Aerodromsko Naselje, or the Airport Neighborhood, right across the street from the Sarajevo International Airport, Butmir, and about a fifteen-minute ride to downtown on a good day. Our street was named after Georgi Dimitrov, a person whose identity or credentials none of us cared to learn. Most streets in Sarajevo were named after fallen war heroes, politicians from the communist era, or famous artists. Our street was long and was shaped like a half oval. From the windows of my room, I could see the airport building, unobstructed in sight, and a tall deep green mountain Igman standing in the background. Growing up, I was accustomed to the windows shaking from powerful plane engines ascending into the sky. The buildings in my neighborhood were two stories high, all well maintained, with colorful flowers in front of every building and many balconies, with leaves and blossoms hanging over the railings. My father had taken care of the building front and planted a couple of roses in each corner of the hedges. A year before the war, he had planted a small cherry tree close to the entrance of our garage and one in the backyard. Our apartment was tiny, about six hundred square feet, facing both the airport in the back and the street we lived on in the front. Amra and I shared a room, whereas the living room also served as a bedroom where my parents slept. Next to the living room was a small kitchen and a dining room, and between the rooms was a narrow hallway with the entrance to the apartment and a bathroom. One could walk in circles, entering different parts of the apartment. And often, when we misbehaved, our parents chased Amra and I in circles until we stormed into the bathroom and locked ourselves behind.

The space did not give any of us much privacy, so Amra and I loved when our parents were at work. We could play music as loud as possible, reaching our neighbors across the street. We often invited our friends over to watch German porn on VHS tapes my father had hid in our brown sectional and giggled and laughed nervously at most obscene images.

The neighborhood was safe. It was mixed as far as nationalities; in our building lived Muslims, Serbs, and Croats. A couple below us, with two children, were a Muslim and a Croat. Across the way from us lived a mixed couple with two children, a Serb and a Croat, and the others were Muslim. Next door lived a couple with two children, one of whom was a girl named Jasmina, a year older than me and who I befriended when I was practically a baby. We moved into the apartment in 1979 when it was first built, so everything was brand-new and fresh. Whether this is a fruit of my imagination or an actual memory, I recall Amra walking me through the living room, placing her hands under my armpits as if she was teaching me to walk. The mustard yellow couch sat on one side and a brown vanity on the opposite side of the room. My parents placed the furniture randomly until they decided on the best location. I was less than a year old, and the parquet stood at a small distance from my eyes. The apartment was our new home.

Back then, the government handed apartments to employees after they were wait-listed, for free. The socialist regime in Yugoslavia gave people safety and comfort. Everyone had equal assets, and competition was kept at bay. Being a good neighbor was sacred. We had Milena across the way bringing sweets every so often; her *marcipan*, a cocoa cake, was the best and well-known among the neighbors. Our downstairs neighbor often checked up on me when I had just returned from school and was home alone. Another downstairs neighbor came to visit practically daily, often just as my mother arrived from work until my mother put a stop to it one day because she was too tired to socialize. The neighborhood felt like a family. And like every family, we had our disagreements, but everyone knew we could count on each other. Being a Muslim, a Croat, or a Serb was never a source of contention; rather, being a bad neighbor was.

The only time an unusual occurrence happened was a murder taking place on our street. A boyfriend of the girl who lived in one of townhouses showed up one day—they were breaking up or quibbling over relationship-related stuff—and in the heat of the moment, he stabbed her with a knife. Her younger brother came in to help, but he was weak and unprepared, so he got stabbed as well. Both died. And I don't know if the murder took place right before we all showed up to watch the police handcuff the murderer and escort him to the police car, but I remember the whole ordeal being peaceful. I was horrified. I looked at the man in the trench coat approaching the police car with his head down, and I was feeling sad about losing the siblings' lives. The shock permeated across the neighborhood until one day; it was gone and forgotten.

My street bustled with kids my age. We played in front of the building and occasionally ventured out to the other parts of the neighborhood. Sometimes we flew on our bicycles, showing off by skipping steps or pushing brakes hard to make a half donut. Jasmina and I were inseparable. We were similar, not only in age but also in how our imaginations came up with endless games that she and I found adventurous and intellectually stimulating for girls our age. When I was growing up, I transposed letters in words, causing me to say *valinija* instead of *vanilija* (vanilla). When our parents gave us money for ice cream, I would ask Jasmina to order vanilla ice cream for me, in fear of mispronouncing it and humiliating myself. She had my back. She and I knew the neighborhood inside and out. Every nook and cranny, where we eventually hid when we smoked at my age of twelve and hers of thirteen. We hid cigarettes in the bushes, and after we smoked half a pack, we went to a grocery store to get gum to cover the cigarette stench before we headed home. While both Jasmina's parents smoked, my parents were devout nonsmokers. If they had found out we smoked, there would have been some serious repercussions. But as the turmoil was growing in the city, I no longer knew how my parents would react to my disobedience.

Some of our neighbors and friends kept saying that war would shift to Bosnia soon, and my parents might have agreed, but they absolutely refused to believe that it could break out in a large city like Sarajevo—a city that was so multicultural, consisting of people with many religious backgrounds. My mother, sometimes wanting my father's validation when she was scared, would ask, "What do you think, Munib? You don't think war will break out in Sarajevo, right?"

My father, calculating his response at first, sitting in his favorite pose with his chin resting on his hand and legs up on the ottoman, gave it some thought and calmly said, "Everything is possible, but it doesn't seem to be that way."

Knowing both of my parents—my father always maintaining his positivity, and my mother getting panicky for the smallest reasons—I sliced their beliefs in the middle and just thought to myself, We will see.

CHAPTER 3

The Airport

War is evil, but it is often the lesser evil.
—George Orwell

GROWING UP, I was not popular among friends. Nor did I strive to be. I was reserved and shy, and my mother was the one speaking on my behalf whether I wanted that. My world revolved around my mother. Almost every night until age seven, I'd call my mother in the middle of the night so I could move to the living room and sleep next to her. As sleepless nights took a toll on her, she took me to a psychologist one day. The psychologist asked me to draw a picture, and I drew a field, blue sky, and flowers.

"Who would you give these flowers to?" the psychologist kindly asked.

With no hesitation, I answered, "My mom."

After a series of questions proceeding with the fun drawing activity, the psychologist concluded that I was too attached to my mother. When I was nine, my mother's sister lost her husband to a heart attack, and my mother resolved to visit her immediately. She packed up bags and found her way to Zenica, a city about seventy kilometers west of Sarajevo. The first night, I got sick with a stomach bug, and while my father was taking care of me, I yearned for my mother. I begged my father to call her so I could hear her voice. Because the call was long distance, my father tried to distract me and console me, but I wouldn't give up. Finally, when he allowed me to call my aunt, I was sobbing by the time my mother came to the phone.

"M-m-m-mom." My words were chopped up from intense crying. "Wh-wh-when are are you co-co-coming back ho-ho-home?"

"Sweetheart, I just arrived. I will be back home tomorrow. Go to bed, and I will see you tomorrow."

This attachment ultimately resulted in me wetting my bed until the age of nine or ten. My mother would put a plastic sheet under a blanket so that my pee wouldn't get to the mattress. She'd come to our room in the morning to check up on me and ask me if I did it again. The heavy urine stench gave it away immediately, and she would gently pull my pajamas down, picking it up at a corner and running to the bathroom to dispose it for a wash.

I would think of my mother as a goddess when I was growing up. Although my father was present in our lives, my mother was the one who practically raised us. She made the rules; she enforced the rules; and she made us accountable for those rules. Her personality was infectious, her work colleagues admired her laughter, and our neighbors sought her company as she was full of energy and joy. She had one of those laughs, loud and distinct, where her last "ha-has" sounded as if someone recorded repeatedly and make them into one long sustained note, extending to far distances. When she laughed at home, I could hear her while playing with my friends on the street.

The attachment to my mother, I later reasoned, wasn't the best thing for me when I was slowly becoming an adolescent. In school, I was a butt of jokes and humiliation daily to the point I eventually dreaded attending classes.

The bullying started when I transferred to another school in the fifth grade. Because in the fourth grade, the middle school assigned me Russian to study as a foreign language. My parents determined English was much more useful and transferred me to another school. But I had to pay a price for this extra advantage: the new school was much farther away from my house, and I had to get up earlier to trek there alone to be in school on time. When I transferred, I didn't quite assimilate with my classmates. A boy named Nikola flirted with me in the beginning and wanted to spend time with me, but I had no interest. I was too shy. And it all started there. He couldn't take the rejection, so he made fun of my Prince Valiant haircut, my crooked teeth, my red shoes and clothes I was wearing, and my last name. Like a ripple effect in fast motion, everybody in class called me names and bully me. Instead of rising above the circumstances and make my situation for the better, I succumbed to them and felt devastated. My grades dropped, my self-esteem was sinking like a heavy rock, and I was getting depressed. In fact, I was so depressed that one summer during school break; I had not once gone outside to play with other kids. One day, my mother sat in front of me.

"Baby, what's wrong? Don't you want to go outside and play with your friends?" I'd shake my head and look anywhere but her. "Is there something wrong? What's wrong?"

I would shrug my shoulders, go to my room, and spend the entire day there alone.

The bullying went on for three years, and every school day was a butchering day. I slowly ceased to talk in a group of people. I was growing more socially anxious and awkward, and I was afraid to hang out with the neighboring kids in fear of them finding out I was that person. The kids in school made me feel worthless. My parents, Amra, and Jasmina never found out what was going on with me. I hid my experience from everybody as if I was trying to protect them from my shame and humiliation. That was my main childhood worry. You'd think that was the silliest thing to worry about, but fear not. I felt like my life was doomed forever. I thought I'd never become confident—a wiseass—ever again and be like when I was a young child.

I was so focused on my own worries that I didn't care Yugoslavia was being torn to pieces by politics and was slowly beginning to die. The most northern republic of the country, Slovenia, went through the motions in 1991 and could prevent war. But right after, as if someone shifted a piece of a puzzle on the map, the turmoil moved south to Croatia, and the war there lasted for months. I didn't understand what was going on, but I felt tensions build even among the kids in school and the teachers. Being a Muslim, albeit never being religious by any means, my teachers, mostly Christian Serbs and Croats, picked on me. If I arrived a few minutes later, after trudging long distance through the snow, they would tell me I couldn't attend the class and had me wait outside for forty-five minutes until the next one. Or my chemistry teacher had me take oral exams when I least expected it and gave me the look of "how dare you not know the periodic table by heart" and failed me. All the bullying from the kids must have rubbed off on the teachers, I thought.

My classmates made it easier on me in the eighth grade. I was more accepted by my peers, as we shared our mutual love for MC Hammer's "U Can't Touch It" and the emergence of MTV. We smoked in the school bathroom, rebelling against the teachers and school principals and betting on whether we'd get caught.

When the tension built, with heavy suspense flying in the air, Aleksandar once came to me and said, "There is going to be some trouble. You may want to escape and leave the city."

I looked at his slim figure, his straight hair looking like a wig covering his pointy face and nose, and I was listening as if he was giving me advice based on a story or a book he had read a few days prior. I thought a little of it as he didn't say a lot more. As everything I had hidden from my family, I didn't tell them anything about what my classmate had told me. Would they believe me? Or would they believe a kid who probably didn't know what he was talking about? Aleksandar was a Serb and didn't seem like a bad kid, but when he shared the warning message, his smirk made me doubt it. And so I ignored him.

Soon enough, the schools closed until further notice. I was

relieved, because Nikola could no longer call me Judy, after a chimpanzee in the Judy and Clarence show, or Adnan spit at my face or Aleksandar kick me between the classes. Inflation was extremely high in the country, and the value of the dinar was plummeting. Toward the end of March, the beginning of April, men in uniform put up and guard barricades around the city. Nobody could leave the city any longer without the permission of those who blocked it. My school wasn't reopening anytime soon, so I was growing concerned about correcting my grades in math and chemistry.

One morning, we saw tanks move into the airport. Lined up like large metal caterpillars, they plodded on the street that separated our building from the airport. The view from our apartment window stretched all the way to Igman Mountain, where the Winter Olympic Games took place in 1984. The tanks were positioned all the way around the city, on top of mountains and hills, which meant the enemy had taken the high ground surrounding the city. They had us in the palm of their hand.

I was six when the Games took place. We rented out our apartment to a couple of Croats while we stayed with our maternal grandmother in a part of the old town, sitting on a hill, named Vratnik. When we returned home, we found a red helium balloon glued to the ceiling in Amra's and my room. I had never seen a balloon like that, so I was playing with it all the time. One day, my mother entered our room and opened the window to let some fresh air in. The wind pulled out the balloon out of the window, flying into the sky like it was happy to be free. I became instantly sad and tried to figure out how to get it back, but I knew I had lost my chance forever. I watched it, and I followed it with my eyes until it became a dot and it finally disappeared.

* * *

The tanks belonged to the Yugoslav Army and there were at least a dozen of them heading to the airport. Soldiers were peeking from some tanks and waved back at us. One soldier gave us the middle finger. The tanks turned left to enter the airport, finding a new home on the field along the road. A few days earlier, the airport was flooded with people who seemed to flee the city. My parents kept thinking the Yugoslav Army was here to protect us from a yet unknown enemy. I started feeling excited about all this suspense. It was like being in an action movie that raised the adrenalin and anticipation but eventually, in my hope, would have a happy ending.

The following day, Jasmina and I walked to the airport to check out the tanks. The airport was one of our favorite spots to play at as kids because we liked the trees lined up along the main street, and there was a large grass field where we picked branches from a willow tree and made baskets out of them. This time, the scene was different. The tanks were positioned in such a way that we could not help but see them. We approached a tank with a couple of soldiers guarding it, and we pretended to be guessing what kind the tank was.

"I think it's a T-90," Jasmina said proudly. The soldier standing next to it eavesdropped and smiled. "And that one over there, I think is a T-80 because it looks smaller." It was the first time I ever saw a tank up close.

"Where do you girls live?" I detected his out-of-town accent. "We live right over there, across the street." Jasmina pointed her finger at our building.

"Do you want to go inside the tank, check it out?"

"Oh, no thanks. We're good." I was growing awkward. Typically, Jasmina and I would go inside the airport, check out the planes, and meet and greet foreigners flying through, but this time, the airport was void of both planes and visitors.

"What are your names?" He insisted.

My gut was telling me not to stay there too long, so we cut the conversation short.

"We really have to go home now." We walked home as fast as possible.

When I came home, I was confused about the new scenery that once was my favorite playground. What did this new reality mean to me? Is the airport no longer accessible to me? Should I fear walking on the grounds where safety was never questioned? Did the soldiers have some ulterior motive when they asked us to enter the tank? Was I in danger? What was going on? I told my mother what went down, and she forbade me to go to the airport again.

When the darkness came, we heard loud blasts across the airport in a part of the city called Hrasnica, right below Igman. From the window, we could see the buildings and houses in flames; they looked like little fireballs from the distance. The tanks from the airport were attacking the neighborhood. We finally understood why the soldiers at the airport were there. Earlier that evening, I watched the movie Jesus of Nazareth. I cried when they nailed Jesus to the cross and made him walk through the village; it looked like pure humiliation and suffering, and that was just about how I felt being bullied by the kids in school. The power went off just as Hrasnica was being shelled. The movie ended too soon, as I really wanted to see the ending of it. Panic came over my mother, so she invited over our neighbor, Jasmina's father, Coco (Tzo-tzo), to see if he knew what was going on.

"C-C-Coco," she was stuttering, "do you know what's going on?"

His perfectly round head with little hair on it and his big brown eyes looked calm. My mother took a pack of cigarettes he brought over, and she lit one in her mouth. She was shaking, along with the cigarette in her hand. It was the first time I had ever seen my mother smoke. I wanted to go for it and grab one to calm my own nerves, but I didn't think my mother was ready for yet another shocking news. Coco had no clue what was going on. Calls to electricity dispatchers didn't go through, as the phone lines were nonstop busy.

"I really don't know. I just woke up," Coco said as he exhaled cigarette smoke.

As the darkness fell, the fire in Hrasnica looked more prominent, and the shell blasts screamed louder. The electricity finally came on around midnight. We went to bed shortly after, clearly not having a slightest of clues about why things that just happened did.

In the morning, the TV broadcast the alarming news in and around the city. Barricades seemed to have been put up everywhere, and it became more and more difficult to get out of the city. By April

5, the enemy occupied all the hills and mountains that surrounded Sarajevo. The airport was shut down—it took some time to get used to the quietness that replaced the loud plane engines. Schools were closed too. On the same day, a shooting occurred on a bridge downtown, and the first victims died from a bullet.

Sarajevo was under siege.

A couple of days later, my neighborhood got attacked from the airport. It seemed like the enemy had strategic plans on which parts of the city to shell and when. That windy sound of sirens, signaling the potential death to come, never arrived. Absolutely nothing hinted what was to come; the air was filled with the unknown and anticipation. Since our building was the first one facing the airport, it became the easiest target. When the shooting began, our neighbors, my family, and I ran down to what we called a basement, which was on the ground level and exposed to the danger from the outside, with only two thin walls separating us from the enemy. My mother gave Amra and me Lexilium, a medication that was supposed to calm us down. We brought blankets since the cold still lived in the early spring nights. The shells were loud, and the building shook when hit. As a shell hit the ground or the building, my body felt like it was vibrating, but then it instantly felt hollow, as if all your insides and soul exited and flew away, leaving an empty husk in profound confusion. The shell blast often caused me to raise my hands to my face as if to protect myself while the ears became deafened and all the noise became muffled.

Electricity was shut off again. We lit candles, and our neighbor from the first floor brought a small battery-powered transistor radio so we could listen to the news.

We heard on the radio that the army had captured a few Bosnian politicians that night, and all they held the phone negotiations to release them live over the radio. Our neighbor was an older illiterate woman who gave us updates on the news coming quietly from the radio.

She suddenly screamed out, *"Puca tenjak sa Vrataca,"* "A tank is shooting from Vrace!" Since she said it grammatically incorrectly,

Amra and I looked at each other and burst out laughing. Lexilium clearly worked. Other parts of Sarajevo were being shelled at the same time.

Someone frantically banged on the front unit door. Fear kicked in, as Amra and I automatically reached for each other's hands, eyes wide open. "Come out!" they screamed.

We had put a long, thick plank across the door to prevent someone from storming in and attacking us. I wondered for a second if the soldiers from the airport might have taken a walk to the building in order to threaten us with their guns and tanks. But why would they? They seemed so friendly, and they even offered us to check out the tank. The banging had become persistent and the voices outside screamed for help. "Come out now! We need your help! There's fire in the building!" We recognized the voices of our neighbors.

We removed the plank to open the door, and outside on the street stood our neighbors, who told us that two units down the street from us were burning. They were shelled by the tanks from the airport. The electricity was out, but we could see everything from the bright light of the fire. People were screaming and yelling while trying to coordinate the bucket brigade in order to extinguish the fire. Adults and children were on their feet, gathering water and passing it along. I helped. Sometime close to dawn, when the sun was rising, we put out the fire. When I went to bed exhausted, the image of the soldier giving us the middle finger from the tank suddenly appeared in front of my eyes. I felt scared.

Our neighbors expressed shock by gathering and chattering among themselves, trying to find answers the following day. The horror we witnessed that night was difficult to accept. How was this even possible? Our neighborhood was friendly and safe. It turned into a war zone in a matter of hours. The two units two doors down from us completely burned down. TV reporters came the following day and interviewed one owner whose apartment had burned. He looked distressed while he spoke in front of the microphone: "I had a large stash of money under the bathtub, and a half stash burned." He cried. "I don't know what to do next or where to go. I've lost everything."

My mother came out and stuck her head in front of the camera to tell the reporters that when Jasmina and I had visited the airport the other day, soldiers had asked us who lived in the neighborhood. People of all nationalities lived in our neighborhood—Serbs, Croats, Muslims, Jews—and they all got along well. Nationality in Bosnia could easily be determined only by a person's first or last name. My mother pointed out to the news reporter the soldiers wanted our names.

My aunt Munevera came the same day to see what had happened. Aunt Munevera was married to my uncle Keko, my mother's step-brother. When Uncle Keko's mother died upon birth, my grandmother adopted him, as no one else in the family had any interest. Keko didn't know he was adopted until he was in his first grade, and his classmate eventually told him. He came home crying, and then my grandmother explained to him what had happened. It was easily apparent to others, as he did not resemble any of his step-siblings either in looks or character. He was tall and lean, and the others were average height with heavy bones. He was often being criticized for being lazy, which none of the others were. Regardless, Munevera and Keko were my favorite aunt and uncle. Uncle Keko always made us laugh with his dry and innocent sense of humor, while Munevera was always so loving and kind. We'd call them and invite them over to visit, and Keko would jokingly say, "Why don't you come visit us? It's downhill for you."

When their son Haris was born two days after my birthday in 1984, I was the happiest cousin ever. I had just turned six, and I was looking forward to having a small buddy that I could take places and read to.

The family lived in a neighborhood close to ours, Dobrinja. Dobrinja comprised five distinct parts, and they were named accordingly. They lived in Dobrinja Three. Unlike my neighborhood, the buildings in Dobrinja stood taller, up to seven stories high, and built in strategic places concentrated along three main roads, with a narrow stream separating Dobrinja Two and Three. When Munevera came over, we walked around the neighborhood to count bullet holes

17

and shell marks that had left imprints, shaped like open roses, on streets and buildings. By then, we knew what type of ammo caused these holes. There was a PAT, PAM, trombone, 105-mm, 120-mm, 155-mm—oh my goodness, 155-mm, so strong! We learned these from our male neighbors who all had served in the Yugoslav Army for one year at eighteen and were deployed to different parts of the country. They learned the lingo in the army, perhaps hoping they would never need to use it again.

Many of the apartments had shattered windows, while some others seemed deserted. We discovered a bullet went through a small window in Amra's and my room and penetrated through the closet to ruin my mother's clothes. As teenagers, we thought it was amusing, as we giggled upon this new discovery.

The mayhem seemed to be present everywhere in different forms. Our neighbors took the liberty of looting one of the two supermarkets in our neighborhood. Jasmina and I joined the mob, but by the time we arrived, they had nearly emptied the shelves. Our neighbors must have been sophisticated in knowing that they would need to gather food and supplies for the tough time to come. My parents took no part in this in their naivety that nothing major would happen, that none of this would last. But my mind was elsewhere. I snatched a couple of bags of *Knorr* soup and a can of whipped cream. The people were grabbing things at the speed of light. Sugar and oil were spilled on the floor, and the glass windows were shattered. It was a scene that one could easily mistake for a robbery. Except, it took place in broad daylight, and nobody came to arrest us.

CHAPTER 4

The Crucial Move

*W*hat a cruel thing war is...to fill our hearts with hatred instead of love for our neighbors.
—Robert E. Lee

MUNEVERA WAS SCARED FOR US. She realized how close the enemy was to the building. While it was peaceful during the day, the nights were filled with terrorizing sounds of bullets and shells. The power was often shut off. She offered my parents to take Amra and me in until it calmed down. We agreed. A shelter was a few hundred feet away from her building, potentially a good hiding place. Our parents wanted to stay at home because they felt they had to safeguard it by their presence.

Amra and I packed a bag with the essentials—a toothbrush, a couple of clothing items, and audiocassettes with the music we liked. We promised our parents we would come home for lunch every day, as it wasn't a far distance and was a leisurely walk. Jasmina came along, but she soon returned home to be with her parents.

Soon enough, all the stores were closed and empty, and we could no longer buy fresh produce. Whatever food we had, that was it. My parents had flour, potatoes, onions, herbs stacked up in the kitchen cabinet, not enough to satisfy our appetites. The bread company in Sarajevo, Klas, sent trucks to different parts of the city to distribute and sell bread to people. The cigarette company did the same. Amra and I went every day and stood in long lines and waited for cigarettes to be thrown to us from a large truck. Munevera and my uncle Keko smoked. And so did Amra and I.

One day, my parents called us to tell us not to come home. Snipers occupied the high-rise buildings in Dobrinja, and they were shooting at the pedestrians from the top floors. Several victims already fell to sniper shots. In one instance, a sniper shot a woman's shoe heel, but not her, as a way of playing with her life. It was a joke we didn't find funny. The telephone lines didn't stop working immediately, but most of the time, I couldn't get through to my parents without dialing multiple times. One time I caught my mother running down to the basement, and in her panicky voice, she told me that the tanks were shooting at the building again and that they had to stay in the basement all day. Since Munevera and Keko lived on the top sixth floor, we had a bird's-eye view of our neighborhood. A lot of smoke was flying in the air. At night, we could see shells bursting in many directions. The power would be out everywhere at night, so the light coming from shells was dramatic and easily apparent. The air smelled like gunpowder; it was so toxic and heavy; I had a hard time breathing. Every night, we wondered what part of the neighborhood was being attacked and prayed that my parents would be fine.

The next day, my mother called us to tell us that our neighbor in the apartment next to ours was shot by a sniper. He died instantly. His mother found him lying on the floor of their apartment, and she came out of the window and wept. "Why did you kill my son? Kill me too! I don't want to live!"

A man in uniform with a long beard and a gun in his hand

standing close to the building laughed and answered, "I didn't kill him. Alija did!"

He stuck out three fingers—a thumb, pointer, and middle fingers —a Serbian sign of pride for the trinity. He was holding a hat decorated by a *kokarda*, a Serbian symbol for *chetniks*, Serbian nationalist guerrilla members that originally formed during World War II and carried on the identity to present.

Mockingly and heartlessly, he spared her life to suffer in silence.

Her son was in his late teens. Every time I saw him, he appeared kind and good-natured, an intellectual of sorts. He was tall and wore glasses, and his unassuming personality made him invisible. He was an only child and lived with his mother. We didn't know about his father's whereabouts. Years later, we found out that the mother jumped off a bridge, ending her life. She never moved on from losing her only son.

After the young man's death, my parents grew more scared and finally stayed at the sister of my mother's place in Dobrinja Five. My other aunt lived down the street from where Amra and I stayed. My parents didn't want to leave home, but they realized it was less and less safe. The day they learned of our neighbor's death, they got up and left everything. My mother came out of the house wearing her blue suit, and when the neighbors asked her where they were heading, she waved and said, "I'm leaving everything behind. I'm going to save our lives."

Amra and I felt good about their decision because we wouldn't fret so much about their well-being anymore.

In the meantime, Amra and I had met Munevera's neighbors, two young men, Anis and Muhamed, who lived on the second floor. We befriended them while hanging out in the basement. The two young men appeared as if they were not cousins in both looks and personality. Muhamed had wavy luscious brown hair and blue eyes, while Anis featured barely any hair and brown cross-eyes on his long face. We often caught Anis playing chess with an older man in front of the building, raising his eyes from the board to say hello and ask how we were doing. You could tell he was out of town when he spoke up in a distinct accent. He grew up in a city north of Sarajevo, Brčko. He had moved to Sarajevo to go to the vet school. After we made our acquaintances, they invited us to hang out at Muhamed's place, on the second floor, where we smoked and played cards. During the day, I would hang out with kids from the neighborhood and toss a ball in a circle. Munevera and Keko lived next to a shelter with a large platform at street level, where kids played volleyball during the day. I was frightened and timid to talk to them, so I would stand close to the circle and wait until they passed me the ball. When the game was over, I would run away fast and go back to Uncle Keko's and pore over a stash of Mickey's Almanacs. Haris was one of my favorite cousins, but he was six years younger than me and was full of rage growing up. While we were staying with them, he was having at least a couple of temper tantrums per day and was unbearable to be around.

Reading Disney cartoons and playing with kids my age made me feel like a young kid during the day. Hanging out with Anis and Muhamed made me feel like a mature, cool girl at night. Anis and Muhamed were older than me, but not by much. Since school was out, we didn't care about getting up early or doing our homework. Both Anis and Muhamed played guitar, so we stayed until late, singing former Yugoslav songs. Muhamed taught us card games, a lit cigarette between his teeth while explaining, and Amra kept winning with her beginner's luck. I never spoke up, but I was in heaven to be around these guys.

Power would frequently go off and on. When it was on at night, we listened to music. Muhamed made an audio cassette of American hit songs. Emina, Muhamed's younger sister, sang to Sinead O'Connor's "Nothing Compares 2 U" and pronounced each word just too perfect for me to wonder where she had learned such good English. She was hoping she would follow her cousin's steps and go to veterinary school.

As time went on, the food at Munevera's was thinning out. It couldn't sustain five people. My mother told us to come to her sister's place. She had enough food for all. We made daily trips for supper and then returned to Munevera's place, where we preferred to be. One day, our parents ordered us to come and stay. It was one of the saddest days for us. The distance to our new home was short—a five-minute walk—but our parents wanted us to be together in the same place.

My aunt Sabaheta was the middle sister among my mother's siblings. While my mother was growing up, learning how to cook, and eventually be a good wife and mother, my aunt took advantage and followed her brother's path of becoming a medical doctor. Among her peers, she was well respected and, along with her brother, had an excellent reputation among other doctors and patients alike. She had married a man from Herzegovina, the southern part of the country. He was a well-educated economist with a strong and distinct out-of-town accent. They had two sons, Emir and Edin, around Amra's and my age, whom Amra and I called Bolek and Lolek, after two cartoon characters who resembled our cousins. Their parents coddled them and raised them to be selfish and self-absorbed. While at work, my aunt was a hero. To her nieces and nephews, she was a terror. When we would visit our grandmother's place, she ordered us around, screaming and spanking us if we didn't do what she said. To avoid her and the spanking, we ran to the backyard, where we didn't think she'd venture. Her husband, Ramiz, was better liked and was known as a fully devout father who would do anything for his sons. As a result, Emir and Edin worshipped him while they often rebelled against their mother, who invoked fear at home as well.

Even when we were young kids, visiting Sabaheta was a dreadful experience. Her place was immaculate, like a hospital, with trendy and expensive furniture in every room and dozens of decorative plates hanging on the wall. When we'd visit, it would be the same old instructions: "Take off your socks. You will get my carpet dirty. Don't run around the house. You will break something. Don't talk too loudly. The adults are talking." Amra and I dreaded living with our aunt and the family, but we could rarely say no to our parents and, in this case, had no choice but to follow their wishes.

* * *

Whether it was a pure coincidence or fate, it was difficult to tell, but the day after we arrived to be with our parents in Dobrinja Five, nobody could peep out of the building or walk on the streets any longer. The hill Mojmilo outside the main street, close to the buildings, was occupied by the enemy, with tanks positioned all over the hill. Danger was imminent. Dobrinja Five, the neighborhood my aunt Sabaheta lived in, comprised only three buildings. Space between two buildings offered a view of the hill, and it was so close that I could clearly see and count the number of soldiers walking back and forth. The enemy also occupied the village next to the buildings. Sabaheta hung blankets on every single window to minimize the risk of being seen by the enemy. I felt as though I was in a coffin: it was dark, with no way to escape. The beginning of May arrived, bringing warmer days. I couldn't stand being home all the time. We had used up all the candles, and after the darkness fell, every day at 7:00 p.m., Sabaheta made us brush our teeth with salt, and then she ushered us to bed after we listened to the news on the radio. Without the right company and some entertainment, we had no reason to stay up. We all slept on the floor, lined up like sardines. Sabaheta would order us to be quiet as soon as we began whispering. Every inch of me hated this, and I wanted to scream instead.

At one point, the running water was shut off too, so we had to go down to the basement and fill water in bottles and bring them to the fourth floor. Since the power went on and off, we were advised not to take the elevators, so we may not get stuck in there indefinitely. Going up and down for someone who was out of shape or who didn't believe in working out was a genuine struggle. Sabaheta added to our struggles, as she panicked so much all the time and screamed at us not to go to the rooms facing the enemy. My mother was always the one who cooked in the kitchen, and it made me mad as if it were okay for her to risk her life.

"You have to cook again?" I'd ask my mom, insisting it was wrong.

"Shhh. It's okay. I don't mind," she replied.

My uncle Ramiz was the calmest. He was extremely resourceful and supplied enough food for all of us to last a month. Since the fridge was out, he put the meat in salt to preserve it. My mother cooked, baked, and grilled everything on the gas stove. She recycled yeast for bread, mixing the old dough with fresh dough. With each loaf, the bread was more and more sour. We rationed each meal and split it evenly among ourselves. The only safe place to eat was the hallway in the middle of the apartment that didn't have windows. Shooting and shelling around the building came sparingly and happened when least expected. To remain safe, we spent most of our time in the little hallway—all eight of us: Ramiz, Sabaheta, Munib, Azra, Amra, Emir, Edin, and me.

One early morning, the shooting was so intense we went down to the basement. Unlike the basement at home, this basement was below ground and was much safer. Boom. One fell nearby. Again. Boom. And again. Boom. Boom. And then it turned into a charade. Boom. Boom. Boom. Boom. Boom...

The shells were relentless. When a shell fell, it felt as if my blood shivered. The aftereffect of a shell falling made my whole body feel hollow. And the closer it fell, the more hollow my body became. They were falling like rain, and they fell astonishingly close. It pierced my ears and made me twitch and jump with every blast. Ramiz took out a couch for the kids to sleep, but there was no way I could fall asleep in the deadly rain. The basement was deep in the ground and was cold and moldy. A few blanket layers kept us warm, but we were sweating like pigs and were wet by the morning. The night turned sleepless. The morning finally brought some peace and rest.

In the morning, a neighbor told us he had counted the number of shells that fell nearby—around five hundred in that single night. Easy to believe. Shells were coming from both the village and the hill.

As time went on, we felt a new tension in the house. Sabaheta was scared all the time; she would sit on a corner sofa, curled up in a ball, and twiddle and pick her short hair for hours. On rare occasions she did speak up, she would scream and yell and take her frustration out on us. Her way of dealing with things in such a dramatic way surprised me, because she was a medical doctor, and I had thought that she was better equipped to deal with death, dying, and whatever else came with it. Ramiz didn't appreciate it when I talked back at his wife, and he complained about my character and offered ways to correct it.

"You know." Ramiz would use his high pitch voice when he was about to make a point and look off into a distance to focus on his thinking. He looked me straight in the eye and said, "You know, you really need to learn how to appreciate and respect those who help you."

I would shrug my shoulders and think there was no excuse for Sabaheta to treat us like we were less. My parents didn't come to my or his defense. It almost seemed as if they had already lost a battle and didn't want to fight. I was livid when I discovered that my aunt's family had used toothpaste and tried to hide that from us. When Edin came out of the bathroom one night, the powerful smell of menthol wafted through the air. Shocked and surprised, I asked him, "Is that toothpaste?"

"No," he'd answer.

"Yes! That's toothpaste. Why are you saying no when I can smell it?" I insisted.

He looked at his mother and father, and they both searched for the best way to address it.

"Enough!" Aunt Sabaheta quickly intervened. "I don't want any fights in the house, do you understand? And remember, this is our home, and we shouldn't be questioned."

We entered another war—a war between them and us. Even my parents felt uncomfortable and unwelcome.

The tension subsided when a neighbor came to visit. Their neighbors across the hallway were a Serb couple, Mileva and Mladenko, who had sent their twin daughters to Serbia. Mileva, a heavier woman with short spiky dark hair and sprouting hair on her pronounced chin, would visit often and tell us how she hated what the enemy was doing to us, and if we needed anything to be sure to let her and Mladenko know. She placed her fingertips on her chest and, with her deep voice, would say, "I swear to my mother, Sabaheta, it's not like I'm bullshitting in front of you."

Sabaheta would morph into an angel and soften her voice. "Thank you, Mileva. I really appreciate it."

But I didn't want Mileva to visit us. She brought this powerful odor—a combination of mothballs, strong perfume, and sweat. It lingered in the house forever since we couldn't open the windows for some fresh air.

A little boy, Esin, and his father, who lost his wife of cancer before the war, lived next door. The man resembled Groucho Marx with his wild hair, mustache, and glasses. He came over every day to give us updates on developments in the neighborhood, and he told us where shells fell: "Well, this morning, there was a 155-mm one that fell close to the building. They were shooting from the village, from that side, though." He'd point at the Serbian village.

He always seemed to know everything. We wondered, How the hell did he find this out? And we'd listen to him with the grain of salt. When he came over with Esin and a shell fell nearby, Esin would put his little palms together, point them to the ceiling, and say, "Ooooo," widening his eyes and putting a surprising grimace on his face. I would hug Esin and give him a kiss as consolation. But I did more so because he was small and cute. Sabaheta couldn't stand the kid. Amra, Emir, Edin, and I made fun of him when he wasn't with us, and every time a shell fell, the four of us went "Oooo."

Sabaheta yelled, "Shut the hell up, kids! I don't want to listen to your damn nonsense. It's not even funny. Enough!" And we laughed even more. Sabaheta didn't want Esin, "that annoying kid," to visit us anymore.

Amra and I terribly missed our gatherings with Muhamed and Anis. In the beginning, we went to the ground floor and smoked cigarettes, but eventually we ran out of all of them, and we had no one to bum from. Having a withdrawal from smoking cigarettes presented another challenge, as if I had nothing to do with my hands or occupy my mind as I inhaled cigarette smoke.

One day, Keko was able to get a call through to Sabaheta for some medical advice. Apparently, the same day, Anis got wounded by shell shrapnel on his left shin when he was crossing a bridge between

Dobrinja Three and Dobrinja Two. The bridge was clearly exposed by a church sitting a kilometer away that had been taken over by the enemy at the beginning of the war. Dobrinja still lacked a functioning hospital or ambulance, so the only way to treat Anis was via phone. Sabaheta spent several intense minutes on the phone, giving step-by-step instructions and explaining what they needed to do to give Anis treatment. My parents didn't know who Anis was, but Amra and I panicked immediately and grew concerned that he might not survive. Through her conversation with Keko, I learned from Sabaheta that shrapnel didn't have to be removed right away. When shrapnel first enters the body, not much pain is felt because of its heat, but when it cools down, the pain worsens. The body could take a foreign object like that and still function normally. I felt relieved that Anis would survive.

From day to day, Sabaheta morphed from an angel into a monster, and vice versa. Her moods roller-coasted to a point when the ride was no longer fun, and it instead provoked much fear of the next turn. While it would make sense to feel empathy for someone's frequent swinging moods, it was impossible for we all faced the same circumstances and fate. I felt all the others maintained their composure as best as they could.

The power was out for days, and we lost a sense of time. We had boiled radio batteries in saltwater to add life to them, but they, too, eventually gave up. The radio was a sacred device to the adults. When the news was on, no one could breathe. We would sit in a circle and listen to the radio and try to make out what came next, what to expect, perhaps an announcement on when all this could be over. But where was my music that I once played loudly through the speakers? How about some of my favorite Yugoslav music, a band namesake of my mother, Azra? I didn't care to listen to the news like the adults did. The teenager in me wanted to blast music and carry on carefree throughout the days. What did I care about the enemy penetrating the front lines all over the country, and what did that really mean to me? All I knew was that I couldn't hang out with friends, smoke cigarettes, walk freely on the streets, and go to places I once enjoyed visiting.

The radio device eventually gave up. It started to crackle and finally died. Boiling batteries in salt no longer worked. With the only source of news cut off, we had no connection to the outside world. A calendar hung on the hallway wall, but we couldn't tell for the life of us what date it was. We took turns in front of the calendar to guess which date it was, turning it into an argument instead. We felt isolated, and fewer neighbors came to visit.

One day, the lights came on, and we screamed in happiness. The power came on after many days. We turned the TV on, hoping to catch a movie or a favorite show. Instead, we saw something else: a massacre on the main street of Sarajevo. The first scene portrayed wounded people crying for help, with limbs cut off, blood everywhere, people crying, keys, wallets, and other personal items sitting on the street. Apparently, two shells fell in the middle of the line of hundreds of people waiting for bread. I couldn't believe it was real, but then I recognized many of the stores and the street I had walked on many times. The two shells killed and wounded hundreds. We all sat in front of the TV, watching the scene with our mouths agape, eyes wide open.

Power went off shortly after again, and we didn't see the resolution to the story. Who did this, and why? What brutal mind could take innocent lives? During the short period the power was on, we realized it was May 28. What we also gathered was that there seemed to be shooting everywhere. Again, we were reminded that Sarajevo was under siege. Dobrinja was under double siege since we couldn't even visit downtown. An entire month had passed, and our feet did not touch the street for any of those days. The danger from the hill was imminent. We had to hide from its sight, or they could kill us. The food was quickly disappearing, and we went to bed hungry more often than not. My parents' clothes were getting bigger on them; their faces were growing serious. My mother's infectious laugher seemed to be gone; she cried often, and the circles around her eyes were deepening. My father kept strong and balanced my mother's sadness, keeping his face stern all the time and reassuring us that everything would be all right, that all of this would soon pass. He perhaps felt that his seriousness and sobriety would balance out my mother's constant panic and worry.

By the end of May, the war in Bosnia was raging full steam. The war permeated all regions of Bosnia, and tens of thousands of people fled the country or became refugees. It was clear the war perpetrators were Serbs who had claimed that Bosnian Muslims wanted a homogeneous country, Bosnia, so the war was a preemptive strike. It was essentially all part of the propaganda that led many Serbs to be brainwashed and turn against their Muslim neighbors. Whatever was happening elsewhere in the country, we had no way of knowing since we lived in our small and confined world of terror. The nearby Serbs shelled us often and with great precision. I would peek out the window, lifting a blanket in a corner, and I wouldn't see a soul on the street. Sometimes, I'd catch a soldier walking on the hill, and I would hide behind the blanket, fearing he might have seen me. Occasionally, I would only see a lonely rat tiptoeing along the building across the street and quickly disappearing into the overgrown grass. The neighborhood was a ghost town. It felt as if there were no other living beings around.

One day, we heard a voice echoing between the two buildings where the view to the enemy side was a straight line, clean and open like a welcoming hug. I realized, except for our own, other people's voices had become a foreign concept. The man's voice traveled along the street until it got closer, and then, in fear of learning what was to unfold in front of us, we peeked through the window to see a man singing and holding a white rag overhead, waving it in the rhythm of his song. I waited to hear a bullet followed by his loud voice, and I pictured him dropping to the street, and then... questions crossed my mind, proving me I was already in survival mode: who would pick him up from the street if shot? How long would he be lying there? Where would he be taken? Why is he doing this? Has he gone crazy? But as his voice dwindled, so did the sight of him. No human voice would fill the silence outside again; only shells and bullets.

More bad news came shortly after. We heard Serbs occupied our home in Aerodromsko Naselje. It was June 17. Early in the morning, around five, the Serbs entered our neighborhood from every which way in tanks and on foot and began ordering our neighbors to come out. They gathered everyone in groups and separated children and women from men. They targeted specific individuals to kill right away, and they killed those who showed resistance right on the spot. There were different concentration camps for women and children. All I could think of were the horror stories of the Nazi concentration camps and the mass murder taking place in them. But later I discovered that most of our neighbors were used for exchange or were eventually released.

My mother connected with Coco at some point, and through him, we were slowly learning about who was killed that morning—our neighbor Husnija, a bus driver, and his mother who lived across the street from us. My father's good friend Fahrudin, who spent a lot of time with him taking walks and playing chess, also was killed. A Serbian soldier shot our neighbor on the spot because he didn't want to leave his home. The Serbian soldiers asked people to take off their jewelry and hand it to them or else their fingers would be cut off. Later we learned that most of these Serbs belonged to a paramilitary group named *Orlovi*, or Eagles, arriving fresh from Serbia. They killed many others that morning, but we didn't hear about their deaths until later during the war. From what we heard, their entire operation was quick. Loads of trucks delivered the people to different camps near the city. Other loads of trucks took the stolen possessions from homes, including ours. I heard that Jasmina and her mother and brother escaped that morning. They walked along the buildings and hid in corners until the air was clear, and they were safe again. Their escape to the next-door neighborhood lasted for hours, what would be a five-minute leisurely walk before the war. Since Jasmina's father was already living in the building of his workplace, they ended up finding transportation to that building shortly after. I was happy that my best friend in the world was still alive.

I was trying to fathom the terror happening at home and recollecting the things we left behind. Oh, was my mother's jewelry still in the drawer in the pink envelope she hid it in? Was Amra's favorite

31

jacket in the hallway closet? Were my favorite shoes with red circles on the sides of the small cabinet? But what about our neighbors? Were they really gone, or was it a hearsay? What wrong could they do to be so casually killed as if they were tiny insignificant pests? What would have happened if we had stayed? Would my father still live? And how would I survive a concentration camp? When justice was at stake, I grew angry. I didn't think anger would have served me well regarding survival.

These strange events were happening so fast that I couldn't focus my thoughts and feelings to reconcile them. None of it was clear to me why all this was happening. My mother cried all the time. And then—so did my father.

CHAPTER 5

New Home

War demands sacrifice of the people. It gives only suffering in return.
—Frederic Clemson Howe

THE CITY BECAME A BATTLEGROUND. The streets and buildings served as borders, building crevices as hiding spots. Other parts of the city—Grbavica, Ilidža, Dobrinja One and Four, among others—fell into the enemy's arms. The east part of Sarajevo was predominantly filled with the Serb population before the war, and the small number of non-Serbs had left when first trouble began. The places Serbs occupied were all strategic places for further penetration into the other parts of the city.

Part of a building in Dobrinja Five, facing the Serbian village, was the enemy line. This same village was the place my old elementary school Aleksa Šantića stood, where many a time I walked through with my classmate and friend Svjetlana hand in hand, in our blue school uniforms, giving away smiles to the women who watched us

33

from their front gardens. It was inaccessible now. A village that mainly belonged to Muslims and a narrow stream, located only a few hundred meters from Sabaheta's building, separated my old neighborhood and Dobrinja Five. A small bridge across the stream led to the village, but the bridge was dangerous and inaccessible because of the exposure to the Serbian village.

We later discovered that the Bosnians formed an army in mid-April. Dobrinja's army artillery was weak and comprised of pistols and an occasional handgun. What the Bosnian Army had was miniscule compared to the arsenal of weapons Serbs had inherited from the former Yugoslav Army—the army that had one of the richest and most extensive weaponry in the former Eastern bloc. When Serbs shelled the streets and buildings, the Bosnian soldiers returned fire with pistol shots that sounded like birds chirping in comparison. It was a deceptive sign to the Serbs to convince them we were armed, sending out a message Dobrinja Five couldn't easily be occupied.

One morning, the Bosnian Army prepared an attack on the Serbian soldiers on the Mojmilo hill. A Bosnian soldier came close to a Serbian tank and threw a Molotov cocktail underneath, annihilating the tank and killing the Serbian soldiers inside. Another tank was captured and was later used for the Bosnian Army's defense. A lot of Serbian soldiers who lived on the hill were killed that morning. I somehow missed the entire thing; I must have been in a deep sleep. The battle took place early in the morning while even the birds were still sleeping. I was later told that it all happened fast. I couldn't recognize the difference anyway, because shooting was shooting, regardless of who stood behind the weapons.

After the victory, Dobrinja Five was no longer exposed from the hill. But the danger still lurked from the Serbian village nearby. To get to our building, we had to cross the street facing the village, exposing us to snipers. In order to give some protection from the village, the Bosnian Army recruited all the Serbs in the neighborhood and had them build a wall made of sandbags that stretched from one building to the other. Even though the workers were clearly exposed to the enemy, nobody was shooting from the village. I stood at the window, celebrating freedom from the hill, and liberated to breathe fresh air. I hadn't walked on the street for months now, and I missed it. Our vacation time was approaching, but I knew any remote thought about planning for it was far-fetched.

Every year, my parents, Amra, and I went to the Croatian coast and spent at least a month there. When I was younger, we went to different places in the Makarska Rivijera—to a little kid, every place looked more or less the same. The turquoise sea dominated in the background while olive and bay trees stood against the whiteness of rocks. There were these purple trees everywhere, and there were occasional palm trees along the beach, kids in their jelly sandals, screaming and enjoying the water, and adults hanging out with friends and chattering with laughter. We often encountered blond Germans turning into lobsters from the sun, the Czechs walking in their socks on the beach, and Yugoslavs from all over the country, making friends and acquaintances. One year, my parents found a secluded place in Croatia—a tiny camp called Broce on the Pelješac peninsula—on which we rented a piece of land surrounded by trees and put up tents that had belonged to us and my mother's brothers and first cousins. It was one of those places where ice cream was sold by a man on foot, visiting our little piece of heaven daily and enticing children with his loud call: "Ice cream, ice cream!" Broce was the place I learned to swim. I was six. My mother's uncle carried me while he stood in water to his waist, and I desperately searched for ways to let swim without fear. When I did, I heard my parents clap at the beach, all smiles. A summer month in Croatia was what I lived for the rest of the year.

Now, small things made me happy. I was excited about the possibility of walking on the street again. When the Serbs finished building the sandbag wall, which was about three feet high, they walked blindfolded along the building toward the village. They were led by a Bosnian soldier on both ends. The same day, I heard that Mladenko, Mileva's husband, somehow died. I heard someone say he was a spy and had a radio that helped him communicate with the Serbian village. That must have explained sudden shell outbursts when several people were on the street. The Bosnian Army conducted a raid in the neighborhood and found guns in Milenko's possession—guns luckily he hadn't used. Mileva wore all black. We went over to visit her, and she cried, holding a handkerchief close to her mouth and staring at a spot on the floor. Sabaheta tried to console her, but mostly, words escaped her.

After the wall was built, life in the neighborhood immediately improved. We removed the blankets from the windows facing the hill, and we enjoyed the view of people walking on the street. My parents still didn't allow us to go outside since it was still dangerous, with shells falling unexpectedly, with no warning. We were better off staying home, even though the sun beckoned.

One day, we all sat in the little hallway when someone knocked on the door. Emir jumped up to open the door. We heard a voice. "Hi, does Amra live here?"

"Yes, she's here. And who are you?"

"I'm her friend Anis."

When we heard his name, we jumped from the sofa and ran to the door.

He wore a bottom uniform and a purple T-shirt. On his shoulder was a handgun. We couldn't believe that he had found us. We each gave him a hug and ushered him inside, big army boots off first. Everyone introduced themselves before Anis sat on the sofa, where we all had a good view of him.

"What are you doing here, Anis?"

"I enlisted in the army in Dobrinja Five."

"Dobrinja Five? Why Dobrinja Five?" someone asked.

"I didn't like how Dobrinja Three Army was organized." He gazed over at Amra.

Sabaheta, melting in the sofa, asked, "How's your leg now, son? Can you walk fine?"

"Oh, yes, *teta* Sabaheta. I want to thank you in person for everything you've done for me. I feel fine now, and I can walk." He exuded politeness and good manners.

Edin, like a puppy sniffing around, patiently waited for a series of questions: "What is the gun you carry?"

"It's a Kalashnikov."

"Oh. Does it shoot fast?"

"Yes. It can shoot rifle and individually."

"Have you shot from it already?"

"Yeah, I have."

"Did you kill anybody?"

Anis laughed. "I have no idea. It gets too dark at night. It's difficult to see anything."

My parents sat quietly and listened to the conversation. My mother's lip twitched, and it made her herpes dance like a wave. Ever since she became homeless and heard of many of our neighbors being killed, she was distant, uninterested in much at all. My father was the same. Most of the time, he was quiet, but now more so than ever.

When Anis was ready to leave, Amra and I followed him to the first floor to smoke cigarettes. The first puff I inhaled made me dizzy, for I hadn't been smoking for weeks. We hung out on the ground floor in an abandoned apartment. A family had left the apartment just as the war broke out and someone broke in and made it a pass-through and a hangout. The glass on the windows was shattered and sat on the floor. Anis had an entire pack of cigarettes; he told us he was getting cigarettes as the form of payment for his army duties. No more dinar in circulation.

After we caught up, I left the two of them alone. It was at that point their love blossomed. He visited as often as he could from then on.

* * *

One day, Sabaheta stood in the bedroom facing the airport, and she screamed, "What's that noise?"

"What noise?"

"Are those planes? I think they're planes!" She lifted a blanket at a corner of the window to figure out what was going on, but she saw no clear visual clues. She thought she might have seen the plane's winglet sticking out and creeping behind the buildings in our neighborhood.

Apparently, a single plane landed at the airport, welcomed like a honeybee by a flower. I thought maybe its sudden arrival signaled the beginning of the end. Someone must save us all and realized that all of this must have been a horrible mistake. We heard something else. The United Nations (UN) deployed food to the Sarajevo people. For an equal distribution to each household, there had to be a list of all residents in the three buildings. Ramiz was put in charge of logistics for civilians in the neighborhood. He had a PhD in economics, and he was good at organizing and anything that had to do with logistics.

He walked around the neighborhood and collected people's names, their age, and a number of heads in each household. Emir and I helped by writing all the names Ramiz collected in a notebook. After living in seclusion, I was surprised to see how many people lived around. The population was quite diverse, but it was mostly Muslims who lived in the neighborhood.

Time came when Ramiz realized that my family and I were ready to live alone, in another apartment. Losing our home gave us the new status of refugees. We were displaced, homeless, nowhere to go in the city the many past generations of both of my parents had been born and raised. As refugees, we had a right to an apartment.

Many people abandoned their home in the beginning of the war and they weren't returning soon. They made their homes available to newly made refugees. Ramiz found us a two-bedroom apartment in a building across from theirs, facing the hill on one side, Dobrinja Three on the other side. Only a street and a small field separated us from Dobrinja Three. The apartment was on the fourth floor. It had belonged to Serbs. The woman, we heard, suffered from breast cancer. When Sabaheta heard this, she gave a prognosis: "I don't think she'll survive in these circumstances. She'll die soon."

Our new next-door neighbor, Ramiza, later told us the husband was a hard-core Serb. "I wouldn't be surprised if he's shooting at us right now. That son of a bitch."

They had two daughters, younger than Amra and I. The whole

family deserted the apartment the same way we did ours. They left everything behind, intact.

We all seemed to be in a better mood when the moving day arrived. We had nothing to move, really. All we had in our possession was a small bag full of audiocassettes. Before I stepped onto the street, my heart was racing. Our mission was to cross the street, while trying to stay alive, show up at the place, and take it over like amid anarchy. I was given the instruction that when I came close to the sandbag wall on the street, to duck as low as I could and run as fast as possible. My feet felt as if they were chained and made of cement. Like a muscle memory, my heart wanted to take me home to the airport neighborhood, but my mind knew this was impossible. Thus, I kept heading toward my new home. When I ducked down, I felt the sun shining on my back after it has been forgotten for months. I missed Croatia even more than it was the beginning of July.

When we arrived on the fourth floor, the entrance door awaited ajar. We slowly pushed the door, only to be greeted by a terrible and heavy stench. Ramiz showed up shortly after and told us the key lock would be replaced because it had to be broken for access. We walked around to check out our new habitat. It did not impress me. The furniture was old, the bed in the main bedroom squeaky and covered with a yellow mustard satin cover. The two single beds in the kids' room were too small for Amra and I. The toys were scattered all over the floor as if they didn't bother to leave any impression that they cared at least a bit. Compared to our home, this place looked like a dump. My mother was known among friends, neighbors, and family for her cleanliness and neatness. As a custom in Yugoslavia back then, she made crochet pieces she hung all over the apartment—on the coffee table, the TV, the radio, the telephone. She had carefully picked out the furniture in both rooms and matched the drape colors with the rest of the decor. She had a green thumb, and her plants bloomed with full colors and blossoms. One year, sansevieria, a plant that rarely gives flowers, bloomed, as if it was a testament to my mother's care. She cleaned our house thoroughly on a weekly basis and did a head-to-toe deep clean of the house on each turn of the season, making sure everything was sparkling and put in place.

Upon entering, she looked around to acquaint herself with the new surroundings and what would be her new and yet unknown home. There were no crochets hung anywhere. The people who had lived here didn't seem to care about aesthetics. The fake paintings hung on the living room wall looked cheap and lifeless. Still, the place had to be ready and cleaned for us so we could call it our new home. The apartment was larger than ours in size—it had two bedrooms, one and a half bathrooms, and it was stretched and long, facing only one side, looking over Dobrinja Three and the hill. It provided enough space for all of us to sleep.

My mother opened the freezer in the kitchen, and within seconds, hundreds of flies filled the apartment. She screamed in surprise and nearly belched. "Ugh!" She slammed back down the freezer door and ran to the living room to compose herself. The freezer was filled with the meat that turned rotten without power. My mother opened all the windows, hoping the flies would find their way out, but there were too many. The refrigerator and the freezer were infested with maggots. I blocked my nose with my thumb and my pointer finger and ran to the other room.

My parents cleaned the house. Amra and I went to the basement to fill bottles with water. A small pantry in the long hallway, stretching between the bedroom and the dining room, had some cleaning supplies. Next to the pantry was a small bathroom, and next to it was a full bathroom. Across the pantry was a small bedroom. The apartment felt like it was a long train, but a dirty and old one that took us nowhere. Even though we could stretch out and feel comfy with three beds and a sectional in the living room, we all slept on the floor of the cozy dining room. Sleeping on the floor was safest and easiest to avoid a bullet. We took mattresses off the single beds and placed them along the small kitchen bar that stood between the kitchen and the dining room.

Power came on and off occasionally, and the buildings in Dobrinja took turns. When it was our turn, we turned on the TV and watched an Eddie Murphy movie featuring delicious food that made us hungry and resentful of a good life elsewhere.

"What the hell!" we would exclaim, followed by laugher. "This is not fair! I could sooo have that hamburger right now."

Each set of buildings got two consecutive hours of power max, then the next one, and then the next one. When the building across the street had power, we watched and stared at the lights with envy as if they were a brand-new invention.

By coincidence, the day we moved, we had power for a couple of hours, so my parents vacuumed and cleaned the place as best as they could. They got rid of all the meat and cleaned the freezer. When Amra and I looked through cabinets and drawers, curious what we might come across, we found a bit of food left in the pantry that we could use.

The view from the apartment stretched to the hill across the main street. We could see the top with the remains of a burned tank. On the left side stood the major intersection, leading to downtown Sarajevo on one side and to the Serbs' position in Dobrinja Four on the other.

People walked up the hill and cut the trees there into smaller branches. They piled the wood on a sled and dragged it behind until their final destination. They used the wood for fire cooking. My parents considered going to the hill to get some wood, but more often than not, they decided it was a bad idea out of fear of being seen from the Serbs' village. Instead, on the top floor of our building, another abandoned apartment someone had already broken into remained open all the time. One day, Amra and I walked up gingerly up the stairs so that no one would discover us. When we arrived, we found the wide-open apartment with nobody inside. The furniture was modern, and the décor seemed tasteful; I almost wished we could live in this apartment.

But when I looked up, I noticed the roof was heavily damaged by shells, and I could see the sky above. Some of the items in the apartment were damaged from being exposed to the rain. We tiptoed slowly, as if expecting someone to jump out from behind the corner to assault us. The same fear took me to the time I was a kid and a family in the building across from mine, a son and a mother, lived in a hoarded, smelly apartment they had kept unlocked twenty-four seven. My friend Svjetlana who lived next door, told us one day they were both gone and encouraged us to come over and check out the place. She, Jasmina, and I mustered up the courage and entered the apartment. Books, clothes, and pots lied on the floor in disarray. Someone told us the son was a drug addict, so I was looking for needles and other tools that would serve as the evidence. I grabbed a purse from the floor to see if it contained any change for ice cream, but the purse was just as neglected and abandoned as the apartment. We had quickly rushed outside, empty-handed.

Fortunately, no one was on the top floor. Amra and I grabbed books and old shoes and anything wooden that would burn. My mother was always looking for wooden items to help start a fire.

A couple of days later, we received our first humanitarian aid: flour, oil, salt, sugar, rice, beans, milk and egg powder, and brown lunch packets, those that were at one point served to US soldiers in Vietnam. A lunch packet contained a pre-made meal in a plastic wrap —the options for the pre-made meal varied from chicken a la king, which I jokingly called chicken a la shit, to pork—matches, a juice packet, chewing gum, small chocolate bar, and mixed dried fruits. Since my family and I didn't eat pork, we often traded pork lunch packets for chicken a la king with our Christian neighbors. Each household took turns to pick up the food for the entire building subdivision, then each family would pick up their ration.

Occasionally, not every time, we would also get Icar, similar to American Spam, processed beef in a can. Rumors went around that someone once found a paw in a can. We'd be absolutely disgusted, but we would still eat the meat. The humanitarian aid didn't comprise fruits, vegetables, meat, real milk, or eggs. Regardless, the size of our menu went through the roof.

Creative people invented recipes similar to those before the war. We had a notebook and began jotting down recipes shared by our neighbors. We gathered multiple recipes for the same item and compared them, deciding which one most resembled the real one. We made multiple versions of faux Nutella, and when we discovered the one that was closest to the real deal, Amra noted it in the book as "closest to the real one." The food was substituted by what we had. Rice was now new potatoes, dandelion leaves were now new spinach, Icar was now new ground beef—pies that we often made with potatoes and spinach didn't quite taste the same. These new flavors skewed our pallets.

If there was one important thing to know about social life in Sarajevo and Bosnia, it would be coffee. Coffee was not just a beverage among Bosnians. The whole social life revolved around coffee. You get together with a friend, you make a strong Bosnian coffee in a small pot, *džezva*, then you pour it into a small cup, *fildžan*. Then you dunk a sugar cube into your coffee and bring the cup slowly to your lips and slurp it and savor the strong taste of it. In between slurps is a conversation that might last for an hour, if not longer. Coffee was gold.

But coffee was nowhere to be found in Sarajevo during the war. All sources had been depleted. Instead, someone came up with the idea of roasting lentils and make coffee with those. My mother succumbed to the idea and roasted lentils that came from humanitarian aid. Once she made coffee, she and my father would sip it, placing their cups on the table, looking disappointed, empty of words.

"Does it taste like coffee?" Amra and I were curious.

"It can pass." They tried to remain positive. The mind was playing its tricks on people and convincing them of new things as normal. My mother made fire on the balcony when it was peaceful outside and made coffee and meals there. She'd take a pan and pile wood and paper inside for the fire and cover it all with bars where a pot with food would sit. When the wind stubbornly kept killing the fire, she would slam the pot against the balcony floor and yell, "Damn wind! I can't cook like this! I can't, I can't!"

She would come inside and sit on the sectional and cry. Once she composed herself, she would go back outside and battle the wind until she finished cooking the meal. It took three to four times longer than if cooked on a stove. It made me three to four times hungrier to wait.

Amra and I found two decks of cards in one of the bedrooms, and we spent most of our time playing solitaire.

Since the power was off most of the time and we used up all the candles, we invented a lighting device that was made of a jar, a cork through which we put a shoelace, and oil used as fuel. We called it *kandilo*, a name I had never heard before. It was impossible to read next to, but it came in handy when we walked around or sat in a dark room. The *kandilo* produced black and heavy smoke, and it made dark marks on the walls. The more lighting devices we had, the better, but we had to cover the windows with blankets. With low light pollution outside, the Serbs could detect even the smallest of flickering lights, exposing us to danger.

During the day, I often hung out at the window between the third and fourth floor of our building subdivision. The windows were glassless at that point but were covered with one-inch square metal bars, so it gave the location for some safety from bullets and shrapnel. I could see the building across the street from which people would occasionally come out and run. A boy around my age would often come out of the building and stand in front of it. He wore a green beret and had legs shaped like an O. He eventually noticed me kneeling on the floor with my fingers entailed in the squared bars. Every time he saw me from then on, he looked up and waved. I became obsessed with him, and each time I saw him, my hand palms sweat, and my heart raced. His father, Faruk, was my mother's neighbor when she was growing up. She knew him well. He came to visit every once in a while, and my mother made a joke about the two of them becoming in-laws. I discovered then that the boy's name was also Faruk. Amra named him Junior for an easier identification in our conversations. He was something for me to look forward to every time I went to the window.

Playing solitaire and drawing became our new hobbies. We drew faces of people we knew and a bubble above their head to write a dialogue, later guessing who that might be. It was a fun game, but eventually we ran out of people's faces and words people were saying. We found a radio in the bedroom and moved it to the living room. My mother wanted us to leave it on at all times so we could tell right away when the power came on. Every time it came on, a patriotic song played. Musicians seemed to be quick in composing them, as these songs were multiplying like flies.

Even though the prospects of having a normal life soon were slim, we felt relieved that we had the space to ourselves and feel like a family again. We had a home. The apartment was comfortable, but its unique stench was clear in giving character to its past owners. The furniture was dated and old. We eventually demolished the unappealing paintings and used them to start a fire.

We were quickly learning how to manage day-to-day chores that involved water and power. When we took a shower, we heated a large pot of water and mixed it with cold water and then poured it onto ourselves, one cup at a time. The water used for the shower was kept to flush the toilet, often unsuccessfully getting rid of all the waste. When we washed dishes, one person was pouring water slowly so that not too much water was being wasted, and another person would rinse them. We'd collect that water and contribute to flushing the toilet. When a guest came, we would kindly ask them to go home and drop waste in their own dirty bathroom. My mother eventually made a hole in the gutter pipe, passing our balcony, using a sharp tool she found in the house. She'd collect rain and use that water to flush the toilet. Any water drop was precious.

Everything in the house looked dirty and unsanitary, which was something we couldn't quite get used to.

My mother cried every day, on a cue, as if someone tapped her on a shoulder and said, "Go! Now!" She looked thin, and her hair looked disheveled, getting longer, flat on the top with curly remnants from a perm on each side. I didn't know what to say or do partially because she never tried to explain her sudden outbursts, so I thought she wanted us to leave her alone to mourn in peace.

Shortly after, the Bosnian Army enlisted my father, who was way in his forties, and not in the best health conditions, to be a front-line soldier. He was given the task of guarding a building that faced the Serbian village, to monitor for any suspicious activity, and to shoot if necessary. He and other soldiers were assigned to a specific place in the building where they would sit there for hours until other soldiers replaced them. By then, the building was completely damaged by hundreds of shells and they looked like abandoned pieces of Swiss cheese. Some parts were burned, but the side facing the Serbian village was completely shelled. That side now served as the frontline between Serbs and Bosnians. The Bosnian Army had protected their position by building sandbags walls.

The Bosnian Army turned an empty apartment on the first floor of our building into a youth club. It served as a place for teenagers in the neighborhood to hang out. Sometimes soldiers visited to shoot the breeze with the kids. One day, the soldier who threw the Molotov cocktail the morning the hill was freed showed up. His name was Omar. He was tiny and looked like a fragile boy with ambitions to become an adult overnight. He wore a ponytail under his beret, boots that looked oversized for his stature, and a green uniform. He always wore a big smile on his face, as if he was never close to death. He came with his best friend, a large guy with a pointy nose, buzz cut, and small lips. I felt small in their presence.

The kids begged the soldiers, "Come on, give us the password." The curfew began every night at ten, and only soldiers with the password could walk on the street. The password changed every night.

"If we give it to you, we'll have to kill you." Laughter broke out. Some girls of Amra's age joined the army and were employed to work in the kitchen. I almost wanted to do the same. I felt I needed to contribute, but I didn't want to commit to a menial job because I had no kitchen experience. In the years of the war to come, we learned that those who volunteered to be in the army at the beginning of the war could not get out of it so easily and were trapped in their army duties indefinitely.

Someone mentioned in the youth club that a Red Cross office was opening up behind our building on the street level. In peacetime, the office was a store, but I didn't know what kind since it was looted and transformed into an unknown empty space in the beginning of the war. Beka, who was in charge of the office, was a short man with dark skin, and he hired me as a volunteer to work there a couple of days a week, or as needed. He smoked a lot and always had cigarettes with fancy brands. I wondered where he was getting them in a time of scarcity.

The Red Cross office collected clothes from the empty apartments, and then the clothes were distributed to refugees and those in need. My job was to count and label every clothing item that was delivered and then type a list of the inventory. The Red Cross office was my outlet to temporary freedom.

Every time I headed over, my mother warned me, "Run as fast as you can. Did you hear me?"

"Yeah, yeah, don't worry."

When I arrived at the store and was about to open the front door, I'd look up at our apartment and see my mother sticking her head out the window. I'd wave, and she'd yell out, gesturing with her hand as if she was whooshing a fly, "Go inside! Go inside!"

A pile of clothes would wait for me on the floor every day. I guess this would have been a perfect opportunity to pick out clothes for myself and my family, now that we were homeless and had left everything behind. Instead, I'd pick through the clothes with disgust and focus on my job, separating bottoms from tops, piling them up by size and color, and then counting them all. I would write it all down on a piece of paper and sit at the typewriter to make an inventory with the description of every item.

But one day, I resented it. While I was at the typewriter, Beka came behind me and drifted his hand until he placed it on my right breast. I jerked his hand away and gave him the look, signaling he better leave me alone. He walked away, and I continued to type on the typewriter as if nothing had happened. That day, when I headed home, I grabbed the typewriter and logged in the inventory from home. I never returned to the office again. When Beka noticed I was no longer showing up, he hired another girl a few days later. Shortly after, when she went outside the office for a smoke break, a shell fell next to her, killing her instantly.

It was an epidemic: every day someone in the neighborhood died.

47

A boy around my age died one day. He had hung out at the youth club a few times. He was friendly and loved to laugh. He stood in front of his building when a shell suddenly fell nearby. He died instantly. Given the high death rate in our small neighborhood, the Bosnian Army swiftly turned the youth club into a makeshift emergency room. If someone was hurt, they were sent to the ER on the first floor before they were sent to a newly opened hospital in Dobrinja Three. The death toll was shocking and alarming. My mother didn't let me go to the window any longer. The risk was simply too high. From then on, we mostly hung out with our nearest neighbors.

Amra and I hung out with two sisters, Lejla and Alica, who lived next to the ER. They were close in age to Amra and me. Alica and Lejla had a mother whose one leg was slightly longer than the other, so she walked as if she was gently kicking a lazy cat in front of her. Their father always wore a wool hat, even when it was hot outside, had a long beard, and wore a pair of thick glasses.

Alica was finishing the fifth grade and Lejla, who was in high school, made her practice fractions. "Alica doesn't understand the concept of fractions." She giggled. "I tried to explain it to her so many times, but she doesn't get it." She giggled again. When Lejla giggled, she was showing her yellow teeth, and she later volunteered the information that her teeth turned yellow because of the medication she was taking. She was a heavyset, and her long flat hair made her look larger than she might have been.

"I'll give it a shot." They gave me a piece of paper and I drew a big circle. "Alica, you see this circle? So this circle is considered a whole. When you cut it in half, you now have two halves, okay? And when you slice these halves into more pieces, you get thirds, quarters, fifths, etc. Let me show you how you can express this in numbers." I wrote a bunch of combinations to show her the concept. But when I looked up, Alica's freckled face was covered in crocodile tears. Lejla giggled.

My attempt to teach her math failed, but we hung out almost every day, and we took turns between our places. One time, we invited them for a cake that we made from a recipe someone gave us. We used crackers and items from the lunch packet to make the cake. Considering we hadn't eaten a cake for months, it was delicious. Time seemed to move more quickly as we savored the cake and suddenly realized Lejla and Alica may not arrive. We wondered what had kept them so busy and why they were running late. Just as we devoured the last piece, Alica and Lejla knocked on the door.

When they arrived, we broke the news: "Oh, we're so sorry, but the cake is gone. We didn't think you'd show."

I noticed disappointment on their faces. "Oh, that's okay. Don't worry about it." Lejla giggled. They seemed to visit us less often afterward.

One day, Ramiz came over for a visit.

"How's it going?" He seemed to be in a better mood since we left his home.

"Things are good. Thanks again for finding us the apartment."

"I'm glad it's working out for you. I'm going downstairs to talk to Izet and why don't you, one of you, come downstairs and I'll give you the paperwork for the apartment. Give me ten."

Even though we were during the war, when no rules applied and even though the owners couldn't come back, even if they wanted, this contract gave us some security. Ramiz surprised us when we learned he had arranged with his neighbor to bring a bag of apples that my grandmother had collected from her neighbor's garden, and he asked us to get it with the key.

The telephone lines were cut off, and we couldn't call any of our extended family members. Before the war, we had visited our maternal grandmother every Saturday. It was a habit my mother had instilled in me since I was a young child. The distance between most of our family members was about half an hour car ride at the most. Now we didn't even know if they were still alive.

Amra and I, both wanting to be on the street level, decided to meet Ramiz there. Anis was heading to the frontline, so he walked with us. When we arrived at the street level, we found Ramiz talking to someone on the street. Anis crossed the street and entered the building across from ours. We stood at the door, with one foot crossing over to the outside world. It was peaceful. I could see the garage on the right side, empty and dark, and a car with a driver inside on the otherwise empty street. I looked up and saw a couple of people looking out the window. Though it felt nice to be outside yet again, the view had become dull, the outside uneventful, so I went inside and stood behind the metal door.

Suddenly, a loud blast came. My ears deafened, and I couldn't hear anything. Amra pulled me toward the stairs, and we ran down to the basement. We stood on the basement floor, and we grabbed each other's hands, squeezing them tightly, and laughed. Another blast came, just as loud as the first one.

She looked at me and asked, "Are you hit?"

"No. I don't know. Take a look." I spun as if we were about to play hide and seek. She examined me. I was fine.

"What about me?" Amra asked. I spun her around.

"You're good." We both giggled.

Through deafened ears, I heard a muffled cry for help. A woman was screaming from her window and asking for help. With hesitation, as if maybe another shell was coming, we walked upstairs to the ground floor to see what was happening. We peeked through the door again, and we saw our uncle lying on the street. A shell shrapnel hit him. The driver who was sitting in a car parked on the street died from a shell that fell onto his lap. He died instantly, his body decimated into a thousand pieces. A few soldiers, including Anis, came out of the building with a stretcher. They put my uncle on top of it and brought him into the ER on the first floor. They carried him past us as if we were invisible. My uncle had his hand right near his heart. He was bleeding profusely. His facial expression revealed immense pain. They took him to the ER, but since he was severely injured, the doctors sent him immediately to the hospital in Dobrinja Three. A heavy woman who was standing on the stairs in front of the ER was knocked down after being hit by shrapnel. They took her to the hospital, along with Ramiz. Anis jumped into the ambulance to help, pulling on the woman's tongue to keep her from suffocating.

She ended up dying on her way to the hospital. Just before I stepped inside again, I quickly gazed at Sabaheta's apartment and saw Emir standing at the window. He saw everything.

Amra and I ran back to the apartment. We told our mother what had just happened. She didn't believe us at first because we still giggled from the shock, realizing we both could have been killed. My mother recalled seeing the ambulance heading fast toward the hospital.

Panic came over her, and she screamed, "Ramiz was hit! Oh my god, oh my god!"

She began walking back and forth around the apartment as if she was disoriented. She took a pill to relax and gave us one each. We knew Anis was with him, so the only thing left for us to do was wait for him to come back and give us a report on Uncle Ramiz's status.

About an hour later, Anis came back. My mother, nervous and impatient, wanted him to speak up and deliver the news about Ramiz. But not a word came out of him. His silence signaled that something had gone terribly wrong.

He finally uttered, "Ramiz is dead."

My mother wailed. That was the only thing I registered, and then I came to a wall and punched it as hard as I could. The pain throbbed from my fist to my arm, but I didn't care. It couldn't have hurt more than my uncle's heart. Anis gave my mother a hug.

"I'm very sorry, *teta* Azra. I'm so sorry." My mother buried her face in Anis's shoulder and wept, sounding utterly helpless.

The city cemeteries were far away and inaccessible, so we had to find a temporary place to bury the dead. A small piece of land next to the garage, sitting untouched, one day became a burial site. Some bodies got buried there, temporarily, until a proper place was established. Ramiz's body was transferred to the city right away. A brave soul drove through the danger zone and delivered his body to a mortuary to be prepped for the funeral. He was buried near downtown. Most of us could not attend and bid Ramiz a proper goodbye.

CHAPTER 6

The Canary

*N*ever think that war, no matter how necessary, nor how justified, is not a crime.
—Ernest Hemingway

THE PHONE CONNECTION was mostly off, and we needed patience and persistence in order to get through to someone. My mother could not reach Sabaheta on the phone, so she headed over to her place unannounced and spend a couple of days with her family. Coincidently, my father and Anis were on sentry duty the same days, so Amra and I were left to stay home alone. My mother had prepared a couple of meals for us before she left. Our parents told us to continue to sleep on the floor so that we would be protected if a bullet came through the window.

The following day, home alone, Amra and I were feeling lonely and lost. We'd persistently call Aunt Sabaheta to talk to our mother. When we finally got through, Edin would answer the phone.

"What are you guys up to?" I'd ask.

"Nothing. Mom's crying. Emir's eating. *Tetka* Azra is about to make lunch."

The following day, again, I asked, "What are you guys up to?"

"Not much. Mom's crying. Emir's eating. *Tetka* Azra just went downstairs to get some water."

The first night Amra and I were alone, the heavy shooting outside startled us. Still shaken from the experience of seeing our uncle Ramiz killed, we jumped up quickly from the floor and ran into the pantry.

The shells were relentless. With no supervision from our parents about what to do or when it was safe to go back to bed again, we felt more scared than usual. Amra was turning seventeen that September and was only two and a half years older than me, but not old enough to be a parent figure. We held each other's arms, shivering.

"What should we do?" Amra asked.

"I don't know. Wait until it completely stops?"

"I guess."

But even my parents were never knew what to do in those circumstances. Nobody did.

My mother returned home a couple of days later, and time resumed at its old, boring pace. I gained a different perspective after our mother left for a few days to be with Aunt Sabaheta and her kids. I felt abandoned and did not welcome my mother, my queen, shifting her focus away from us.

Amra and I continued spending most of our time playing solitaire and drawing pictures of our neighbors and guessing who it was. We thought of people from before the war and would think of things they once might have said. It was the opportunity to recall people we once interacted with regularly and recollect fond memories of the past. When Anis had a night off from sentry duty, he would keep us company and play guitar in the evening. We spent a lot of time in one bedroom where we talked, sang, and smoked cigarettes.

The summer of 1992 was unusually hot. It didn't rain for many days, and the grass was turning yellow. The heat made it easier for us to feel less guilty about not going outside. My mother usually cooked meals in the morning to avoid the afternoon heat.

One day, we were sitting in the living room, and it was quiet, hearing only occasional bullets in the distance.

Amra suddenly jumped from the sectional and yelled, "Look at the bird on the railing!"

A yellow canary on the balcony railing stood out against the dull colors in the background. Just as Amra spotted the bird, Anis knocked on the door, returning from sentry duty. Amra told him about the bird as soon as he set foot inside the hallway and began pleading that he somehow captured the bird. Anis tried to explain he was too tired to dedicate himself to that task, but Amra was persistent. Anis eventually gave in, and he opened up the balcony door. He slowly approached the canary, extending his arm and hand as if he was feeding it. The bird was making small steps back and forth along the railing, but stayed put. Fortunately, shells ceased falling for the time being, which helped to tame the bird. Anis was successfully getting closer to the canary while the bird was slowly approaching the living room. It took about ten minutes for the bird to follow Anis's steps, and after it finally entered the apartment, we closed all the windows and the balcony door.

Naturally, we didn't have a cage or bird food, but our neighbors—an older couple, Stjepan and Emilija—on the second floor had a couple of birds and lent us a cage and some food for the bird.

When we were kids, my parents weren't so big on having animals at home. When I was in the second grade, Amra and I convinced our parents to buy us a couple of goldfish. And they did. Along with the fish, they bought a small round aquarium with pebbles on the bottom, a little grass sticking out from the pebbles and a small net we used to catch the fish when we had to change the water and place them temporarily in a jar. We fed the fish twice a day. Mostly, having these small creatures was quite uneventful. Sometimes, because the aquarium was so tiny, they'd just sit in one spot and not move for hours. I thought they were dead. They might as well be living in that tiny space. They would only show a sign of life when we dropped the food.

One year, when we went to Croatia for vacation, we asked Jasmina to take care of our fish. The family had had multiple stray cats visiting their apartment, so we knew they could take care of pets. When we returned from Croatia, the fish came back to us a couple of days later. Apparently, Jasmina became attached to them and was having a hard time with separation, so we transitioned the move slowly. The day after we got our two fish back, we noticed one of them missing. We looked for it everywhere. We checked every single inch of the floor, every small crevice of the kitchen, every odd space in the house where the fish might have miraculously swum to. Nothing! Could it really be that the fish had committed suicide? Was it really possible we were horrible pet owners? Did the fish miss Jasmina that much? Shortly after, the other one died, and we didn't bother replacing them. Until one day when my father came with a pigeon in a cage.

He had told us that a white pigeon kept landing near his mother's house and was searching for food. Pigeons were common in Bosnia, but white ones were an attraction, unusual. Since he presumed it would make us happy, my father found a cage somewhere, shoved the bird inside, and brought it home. Since the pigeon wasn't suitable for home environment, we had kept it in our basement with all the chopped wood lined against the wall and items that we didn't use often or ever, like a pair of skis and boots that my father found and kept in case Amra or I wanted to learn to ski. We had named the pigeon Gugo, and we went downstairs to feed it bread every night. As I opened the door, I had to be extra cautious as Gugo sometimes flew wildly in that small area, and its flapping wings would make an enormous noise between the bare walls. I'd just drop the food and close the door as quickly as possible so that the bird stayed inside. Several days later, my mother complained to my father that the bird started shitting everywhere and we'd be better off letting it go. He went downstairs the following day, opened up the basement window, and Gugo flew away. We had Gugo for about a week.

* * *

Our new canary seemed to have been happy in its new home. We assumed that someone must have let it go, because it was becoming more difficult to own pets when food was scarce. We kept it outside the cage most of the time. It flew freely around the apartment, sometimes landing on my head and playing with my hair, or on the sectional, jumping and walking around on the furniture. When the time came for us to sleep, we'd put the bird in the cage in a different room, covering the cage with a rag so it could sleep. Most of our neighbors who came to visit enjoyed the bird. Stjepan and Emilija, who rarely ventured out to the floors above theirs, showed up to see the canary. Emilija, an older lady with long white hair and a hump on her back, grabbed the bird gently in her hand and kissed its beak.

She fluttered while speaking. "Oh, you're so pretty. So pretty. I like your yellow feathers. Look, Stjepan. He seems so domesticated and tamed."

Stjepan would be just as in awe. I found it amusing since Stjepan was a world-renowned journalist and sounded and looked smart and overly confident. Seeing him cooing to the bird warmed my heart.

The canary seemed to have been well trained. It never disposed of any waste in the house and would do so only in the cage. There was no question now that it had belonged to someone. Amra took all the credit for owning the bird because she spotted it on the balcony railing. She considered it hers now.

Lejla and Alica overheard we had a bird and came to visit. Our next-door neighbor, Ramiza, would show up every day to listen to the canary sing. It liked to sing, and it sang beautifully. It gave our gloomy days more brightness, hope, and joy.

On September 12, Amra turned seventeen. The day before, we baked a cake for her, and like any other food recipe during the war, this one was improvised. Fortunately, Anis had the day off from sentry duty, so he was going to play guitar for us that night.

That morning, the shells were pouring like rain. Several fell a distance away, and a few fell next to our building. It woke us all up.

Lying on the floor, sleepy yet scared, we listened to shells fall for about an hour until the attack finally stopped. We woke up on a sunny morning for Amra's birthday. Like every morning, we ran to the other room to take the bird and move it to the living room and release it from its cage. When we removed the rag from the cage, the bird was lying dead on the bottom of the cage. Shocked by the bird's death, we all cried. The lovely songs that the bird gave us were gone. We tried to guess why the bird died. We concluded it must have suffered from a heart attack caused by morning shells that fell near the building.

The same day, we returned the cage to Emilija and Stjepan, mainly because it was too difficult to be reminded of the loss. The slice of happiness that the bird brought lasted for about a week. We carried on with Amra's birthday celebration, but with my uncle's recent death and now the bird's passing away, any attempt to truly celebrate was in vain.

CHAPTER 7

❧

Vratnik

*E*very gun that is made, every warship launched, every rocket
fired, signifies in the final sense a theft from those who
hunger and are not fed, those who are cold and are not clothed.
—Dwight D. Eisenhower

To LEAVE Dobrinja Five and go downtown, civilians had to request
release from the Army. The Army was conducting its own confine-
ment regimen, as if more people staying in the neighborhood would
have made any difference. I alone made no difference, and I certainly
couldn't stand a chance to defend us if the enemy occupied the neighborhood. When I applied for my release, the Civilian Office, an Army
branch, handed me a sheet of paper, a questionnaire of sorts, that
asked for the basic information about the person requesting release
and dates of departure. Soldiers were frequently going downtown,
and a civilian could tag along to be dropped off at their destination. A
car would leave once full of passengers after the pickup took place in
the nearby garage. The only way to get out of the neighborhood was

to drive by the Serbian village on the main street. The driver would drive as fast as humanly possible and instruct everyone to duck to avoid being shot.

Summer was slowly slipping away, and colder nights were settling in. The heat didn't work, and electricity was still rare. With nothing to heat the apartment, it became clear to my parents that at least one of their children should attempt to escape Dobrinja and live with my maternal grandmother in an Old Town neighborhood, Vratnik. Aunt Sabaheta, Emir, and Edin had already left the neighborhood to live with my grandmother. My parents decided they would send me for the winter, because my grandmother had the means to heat her home. We requested my release from the neighborhood, and a couple of days later, we got the official stamp of approval. I was growing excited to be reunited with my extended family. I had not seen them or spoken to them since the war began, which was quite different since I used to see them every Saturday before the war.

My aunt's neighbor offered to give me a ride to Vratnik. The neighbor was a soldier whose son had just died. The boy was nine and died when he was playing on the street in front of his building. Like most previous victims, he died when a shell fell suddenly and killed anyone nearby.

The soldier came to pick me up in the morning, and my mother asked him how he was doing.

"I go to the bathroom and I take his clothes from the hamper and smell them. I still can't believe that he's gone." He cried, and my mother cried with him.

I was excited that I would walk on the streets again. A car was awaiting us in the garage, like planned. On my way to the garage, I saw Beka. "Hey, where's my typewriter?" I didn't even look at him.

"It's in my house. Go get it," I told him.

I said goodbyes to my parents and Amra, not knowing whether we would see each other again. The car left the garage, and as we approached the main street, it sped up. Everyone in the car put their heads down in case the shooting began. Fortunately, there was no shooting. Once we finally left Dobrinja, we were in the clear. The other side already felt safer. As we approached downtown, it was getting quieter and quieter, with fewer bullets and shells falling on the streets. It was clear to me then that Dobrinja was the most dangerous part of Sarajevo, with the highest mortality rate during the war.

Driving through Sarajevo was yet another story. Every store was closed. A few cars drove on the streets, many buildings damaged, trash everywhere, and some put on fire, as it was the only way to get rid of it. The trams were sitting on the tracks, abandoned and burnt. People found a new way of transportation—by foot. Overall, the city looked sad amid the war.

I arrived at my grandmother's place safely, with no trouble. My grandmother, ever since I had known her, looked the same. She always wore *dimije*, baggy pants and a top to match, similar to what all old Muslim ladies wore. She had a scarf on her snow-white hair, with a thin braid in the back I had rarely seen. Throughout my life, the only visible thing that changed about her was that she was getting shorter, and she had grown wrinkles on her face over the years.

She was a tough lady, in every sense of the word. When she cleaned her house, she moved the sizeable pieces of furniture all by herself. Almost every Saturday, she'd gather her family, five kids and an adopted son, and all the grandkids. She had thirteen grandkids. With little help from her daughters, she would feed all of us. She had a great sense of humor. When the kids sat down at the table to eat, she'd look at us and say, "I cooked that meal in my underwear."

We'd drop the food to the plate and say, "Ewww, nano!"

"What?" She'd laugh. "Wouldn't you cook your meal wearing underwear?"

A year after I was born, her husband, my grandfather, died of a heart attack. He left no memories for me to cherish. He was a Boehm, as someone once said, stopping for one or two after work and coming home late at night. My grandmother was a stay-at-home mother, taking care of her kids. She never worked. When my grandfather died, she didn't remarry and, as far as I knew, had no romantic interests. Mostly, she spent her time alone unless a family member or neighbor visited or she visited them.

We teased her one time: "Nano, do you want us to set you up with Blake from Dynasty?" We watched the soap opera religiously and thought the actor John Forsythe would fit the bill for my grandmother. She'd sit in a corner of her hard couch, her hair covered in a scarf, smile coyly, and say nothing.

She was as sharp as a razor. One time, all her kids—two medical doctors and three professionals—sat around the room, and someone had to multiply two two-digit numbers. My grandmother was the first one to come up with the answer.

* * *

Vratnik sat on a steep hill, several kilometers away from the old town center. It was so steep that my aunt, one time before the war, blasted down the hill in her small Fiat in the highest gear, unable to switch to the lower one while driving, and ended up crashing into a house at the bottom of the hill. Past the bottom of the hill was the old water pipe, Sebilj, where people fed the hundreds of pigeons, and where pretty cobblestone streets and mosques' minarets stood out. My grandmother's house was on a relatively quiet street with an elementary school up the hill, separated by stonewall and a fence. Along the street were walnut trees, after which her street got the name—Under Walnuts. It was different this time. The little corner on her street where kids used to play all the time was empty and void of human interaction.

Before the war, my cousins Aida and Amina would greet us as soon as they saw my father park his tiny yellow Fiat on the street next to the wall. Not this time. The house looked as if it was deserted. The lilac tree in a corner of the front yard seemed to have dried up and looked lifeless. The front metal barred gate looked like it was corroding, and the water pipe next to it was now useless. The cherry tree in the backyard suddenly gave up on flowering and growing the fruit.

The roof on her house had a couple of holes from shells and was now covered in plastic sheets, with the blue UNCHR name across. The sheets were part of the humanitarian aid for every household, as losing glass on windows from bullets and shrapnel seemed inevitable, especially for lower floors. People would install sheets on the windows by tightening them hard so that it would appear as if it was glass, albeit not being able to see through. The UNCHR sign would stand out.

In peacetime, my grandmother occupied the first floor while the second floor was occupied by my mom's brother Uncle Muhamed and his wife, Šefika, and their two daughters, Aida and Amina.

My uncle Muhamed—or Hamo, as we called him—was born with a cleft lip. As long as I had known him, he wore a mustache to cover the scar. Next to Uncle Keko, he was my favorite uncle, as he liked to joke around with the kids. Before the war, he made frequent trips to Hungary to buy merchandise he would later sell in Yugoslavia. He'd come back with gifts for his nieces and nephews, and we'd be in awe of items that came from outside Yugoslavia. One year, he brought a pair of snow-white skates for Amra. When he was distributing presents, I was waiting patiently to see what he had brought me, only to discover that, like the previous times, he brought me a tiny soap bar from his hotel room. I pretended I was grateful, but as a kid, I felt neglected and sad. It was especially hard when they all laughed about it.

Before the war, my uncle was diagnosed with throat cancer, and he had been treated to full recovery, except his voice had changed and it now sounded raspy and worn out even though the doctors told him he could never speak again. It was one of the most trying times for my mother's side of the family. He was the first person in our family to be diagnosed with cancer and go through the uncertainty of survival. When he was about to be released from the hospital, Šefika was caught playing music and singing as loudly as possible, and when my grandmother heard about it, she was livid. She vented to everyone in the family, and they thought Šefika went crazy, but all she wanted to express was happiness for her husband's arrival home.

Considering what Uncle Hamo had gone through with cancer, he didn't have to enlist in the Bosnian Army. Instead, he was recruited to perform civilian duties much more manageable for his health conditions.

After the shells damaged the roof, they all moved to the basement and live there for the time being. The path next to the lilac tree led to the backyard where the apartment was located. My parents lived in the basement apartment when they first got married in 1974. It had two small rooms and an even smaller hallway where they kept a stove. The bathroom was in the front yard, but if you wanted to take a shower, you had to borrow my grandmother's bathroom. Upon my arrival, there were nine of us living in this tiny space.

Like my family home in Dobrinja, my grandmother's household rarely had electricity. Running water was even more rare because the neighborhood was on a steep hill. The basement was extremely damp, and it was the place where I had developed asthma. I was allergic to mold, and the basement was full of it. At nights, I couldn't breathe, and also, my aunt and my older cousin snored every night, which made it even more difficult to bear nights.

The reunion with my family wasn't as loving or exciting as I had wanted it to be. Except for my cousin Aida, one year older, everybody in the family seemed to have lost the spark in their eyes and the joy and happiness that I had experienced with them before the war.

Aida was often a loudmouth and, as we would say, "had no hair on her tongue." She shared her views and opinions of everything and everyone like she was giving out candy, and people did not appreciate her brutal honesty. At school, kids made fun of her because she had a unibrow, and she'd come home crying, complaining that she was called *sova*, or an owl in Bosnian. Her father, my uncle Hamo, showed up at school one day with his own unibrow and threatened the kids he would kick their butts if they called her names again. But nothing changed. Her loud voice and laughter were infectious. Amra and I enjoyed spending time with her at Grandmother's every Saturday, even though we were annoyed at her for making obvious grammatical errors. She often mixed up č and ć, and we'd try to teach her the difference between the two letters. When Amra had a crush on the singer of a popular Yugoslav band Plavi Orkestar (Blue Orchestra),

Aida, Amra, and I constantly dialed his number until he picked up so we could hear his voice or say how much we loved him. We'd call each other afterwards to find out if there was any success in reaching him and what had transpired from the experiment. The phone bills skyrocketed, and Hamo and my mom found the lock for our rotary phones so we could no longer dial numbers. But the crafty kids in us found a way to dial numbers by quickly tapping the hang-up button, digit-by-digit, until a call went through.

Aida had a mean streak in her. One day, when we were all hanging out at Grandmother's place, her mother, Šefika, wanted to sit down on a chair, and Aida grabbed it and quickly moved it away from Šefika's path so that all two hundred pounds of her fell on the floor. Aida was bent over in laughter, holding her hand to her stomach while her mom was trying to prop herself up with tears in her eyes. My grandmother kicked her out of the room, yelling at her and advising that she had better think about what she had done.

My grandmother, the extremely strong woman who kept us all on our toes, the one who could multiply two two-digit numbers in a matter of seconds even in her seventies, cried like a baby every day and kept complaining about the conditions we lived in. She was born in 1913, just as World War I began, and she had survived World War II, but she had seen nothing like this before, she said. And perhaps, now that she was in her eighties, her age may have amplified the harshness she had to endure.

My aunt, Hamo's wife, Šefika, was the designated cook for the whole family. She prepared all the meals and baked bread daily. At each meal, we all sat on the floor, since we didn't have a table, and divvied up the daily rations. My favorite meal was feta cheese spread on freshly baked hot bread. It wasn't too nutritious, but it kept me full for longer periods of time. Of the five children in the household, three were teenagers and growing up fast, with full and healthy appetites. But the rations were small, and I went to bed hungry every night. Sabaheta often pleaded to give her children more food because boys needed an extra boost to be strong and nourished. I would look at her with contempt and try to control my anger to not say something that would instigate her. I'd be reminded of the days we spent at her place and the toothpaste smell wafting through the air in the night while they made my family brush our teeth with salt. How dare she! I was just as in need of nourishment as they were.

One day, Hamo brought up that Emir spread too much feta cheese on his bread. Emir defended himself by pointing a finger at Šefika, and Šefika did the same in return.

I interjected and told everyone, "Frankly, I think Grandmother uses too much feta cheese."

My grandmother was the only one who wasn't laughing when I said that. We constantly bickered and complained about the smallest of things. Deep down, the person whom we claimed to be the queen of the family, my grandmother, I saw as a distant member—a survivor with whom I competed for resources. I felt she had no interest in using her status to ensure equality among all. It was time to fight for survival and no time to think of the familial hierarchy.

My aunt Sabaheta remained critical, but she wasn't as panicky anymore, because Vratnik was much safer than Dobrinja. She, Emir, Edin and I were retelling some stories about what had happened in Dobrinja and what types of conditions we had lived in, but the others had a hard time believing our stories. Even though the war raged throughout the city, the people living outside of Dobrinja seemed to live a more bearable life.

At night, we would sit in a circle in the smaller room and recount stories about our lives in Dobrinja. My uncle Hamo dismissed them right away, often saying, "I don't believe it. I think you're exaggerating."

All of us, in unison, would yell back, "Yes, it is true!"

"Well, why didn't you go to a nearby shelter if it was that bad?" my uncle retorted, as if to prove us wrong in our own convictions.

"What shelter?" Sabaheta laughed sarcastically. "By the time we got to a shelter, we would be killed several times. Eleven people in my building subdivision alone died over a course of two months!"

At night, we had each other and our stories, whether they were believed or not. When I recounted how Sabaheta treated me and my family, she would defend herself by blaming me for being ungrateful and rude. The conversation would intensify quickly, with both of us trying to prove our point, until I finally blurted out, "You were worse than the war!"

I spoke such words so freely in front of both my grandmother and aunt, the people I learned to show the utmost respect as a child, because I felt that justice would be held in my own hands. Being away from my parents, I felt I needed to advocate for myself, whether that meant disrespecting or offending someone three or four times my age.

Who was I becoming? I did not know.

But that I missed my family was clear as I cried at night and dreamed of their presence. At one point, we established a telephone connection with Stjepan and Emilija, the second-floor neighbors in my parents' building. Their telephone line worked because Stjepan, as a journalist, had to communicate with the world. Often, it took several times dialing the number until we established the connection. Stjepan or Emilija would run to the fourth floor and tell my mother or Amra to come downstairs and receive the call. Almost every time we spoke on the phone, they would tell us about all the people who died in Dobrinja. The soldier who gave me a ride died on a battlefield shortly after gave me a ride to Vratnik. He left behind his wife and daughter, Melina, who would later become a good friend. The family was cut in half in less than a month. The news was shocking. On another occasion, my parents informed us that Faruk Senior died in a recent battle. The soldiers in Dobrinja attacked the Serb positions in the village, and with almost every attack, there were casualties, people we called our friends and neighbors. On a third occasion, I learned that Beka from Red Cross was in a car with a colleague and when shooting ensued; the driver lost control of the car and drove into the Dobrinja stream at a high speed, leaving himself injured while Beka died instantly. It was heartbreaking to have the news delivered. I feared for my family and especially my father, who served as a soldier even though he wasn't fit for it.

All of this made me miss and be concerned about my family even more. Part of me enjoyed being able to walk outside, which I hadn't done for months prior to my arrival. Aida and I ventured out and went downtown regularly. Since the massacre back in May, no major shelling had taken place in downtown or Old Sarajevo until the City Library was shelled. The library stood on the main street, next to the tram tracks and the Miljacka River, a symbol of the city that contained thousands of ancient original scripts. On August 26, 1992, before I arrived, it was targeted and shelled from the nearby mountain Trebević until it completely burned to the ground. Uncle Hamo and Grandmother, who lived not too far from the library, told us that the burning papers flew, and that some of the burnt pages reached their neighborhood on the hill.

* * *

Running water seemed to be an issue across the entire city during the war. The combination of no running water and no electricity made it difficult for us to take showers. We did it once every two weeks, if lucky. In between, I could clearly see the dirt on my skin, coming from soot of wood fire. We would heat a few buckets of water until it boiled and then mix it with enough cold water to take a shower. We'd use a hard soap for washing both our body and hair; the soap was called *kabash*, one that we jokingly said could cause injuries with its sharp corners. It was rather large, the size of an adult palm, and had a strange stench. It was used for laundry many years ago and was the cheapest soap on the market. We'd shampoo ourselves with the *kabash* first, and then rinse the soap with the remaining water. During the rainfall, we would put buckets under the gutter to collect as much water as possible. I was never a huge fan of rain, as it bred melancholy inside, but those rainy days came in handy, and I was happy that it saved us a trip or two.

My paternal grandmother lived across the street from the library. Since her house was at a low altitude, she had running water most of the time. Aida and I visited my grandmother's place every other day or so. We would bring several empty five-liter canisters by carrying them in a wheelbarrow. We'd stop at my grandmother's house to say hello, and my cousin Lejla would greet us, giving Aida a kiss and completely ignoring me.

"Why don't you give your cousin a kiss?" Aida was clearly upset. Lejla shrugged. She didn't know.

I did not feel close to my paternal family. My father had two sisters who never married, a brother who got ill at his age of eighteen, and an older brother who my father did not get along with at all. The older brother, also Uncle Muhamed, was a cynic, quick to criticize whoever crossed his path. When Aida and I came to visit one afternoon, he was sitting at the kitchen table, slurping soup that my grandmother had made for him. He'd quickly bring the spoon up and down from the bowl to his mouth and make a furrowed brow to say with his nasal voice, "What's with your soup, Mother? It tastes like dirt."

My grandmother would look at me, sweetly smile, and say nothing. She offered us soup, but we declined, as I rarely felt comfortable in Uncle Muhamed's presence. He was not a warm and fuzzy kind, and it appeared his daughter, Lejla, wasn't either.

After Aida and I fetched water at my grandmother's, we would roll the wheelbarrow full of canisters up the hill. Since the trip was around three kilometers one way and mostly uphill on our way back home, we tried to carry as much water as possible, so we would only go as infrequently as possible. Pushing the wheelbarrow on the cobblestone streets produced a vibrating motion, making us stop frequently to recover from the nuisance. We didn't always have the strength to push. When we stopped, huffing and puffing, we'd look around anxiously, hoping the Serbs wouldn't see us from the mountaintop and shoot at us. We often rested where the hill was steepest— specifically the place where a cemetery grew bigger day by day. In many places in Sarajevo, open grassy fields became cemeteries, as they were quickly covered with wooden headstones, which in peacetime would have been made of white stone.

We washed laundry rarely, preserving our precious water. On rainy days, we used the collected rainwater for laundry. Clean clothes were not a top priority for us. In fact, the laundry washing was done so poorly that I had strange rashes on some parts of my body. It was uncomfortable, but not impossible to live with. Ironing clothes? Forget it! Before the war, we ironed not only shirts, pants, or skirts, but we ironed underwear, bedsheets, handkerchiefs, and whatever we put our hands on. It was a chore that went on forever and now was completely ignored during the war. At least it saved us some time.

By the end of September, the days were getting colder and shorter, and fall was surely coming along. As my family and I had lost our home and everything in it, I only had a pair of purple sneakers worn from walking down and up the hill often, a pair of jeans, and a light gray shirt. Aida, who was close to my age, gave me a couple of her clothing items. The school up the hill from my grandmother's house was partially turned into a humanitarian aid office called Sumeja that gave out shoes and clothes to refugees. I found a black pair of shoes, pointy at the end, that made me embarrassed wearing them. They definitely weren't my style, and I would have never considered wearing them before the war. I also received a jacket which, when worn, was mismatched with the rest of me. But I had no choice. It was getting colder, and my feet were getting wet in the sneakers full of holes.

During our walks in the neighborhood, I discovered that a young man who I met before the war lived nearby. A year before the war, Jasmina and I went to a concert of a Yugoslav rock band, EKV (Ekatarina Velika) and met a couple of young men. One introduced himself as Adnan. He had long blond hair, blue eyes, and was pleasant to talk to. I had a crush on him right away. To get him to take an interest in me, I had lied and said that I was already in high school, even though I was still finishing elementary school, and that I studied arts. Jasmina had told him she was in her sophomore year of high school, even though she was only a freshman. He was older, but not much. I hadn't realized that he lived close to my elementary school, so one day, while I had my school-books in hand, I unexpectedly ran into him. He asked me what I was doing there, and I was caught off guard, but I must have told another lie again.

When I ran into him for the first time during the war, we stopped briefly, said hi to each other, and exchanged a few words. I was trying to hide my shoes, as their pointy ends were staring at me while I tried to concentrate on my conversation with Adnan. I wanted to end the conversation as soon as possible and continue on my way. While living in Vratnik, I wrote letters to Amra and sent them with a soldier who passed through my grandmother's neighborhood. When she read my overly enthusiastic letter about seeing Adnan and feeling the flare for him all over again, she responded with her familiar handwriting: "Don't get too carried away." I ran into him one more time on the main street downtown, but we only said hi to each other and kept walking. Boys weren't a priority for me then. I might have had a big crush, but I did not know what to do with it. I kept my feelings to myself, especially after reading Amra's letter.

CHAPTER 8

Cookies

*W*ar: a massacre of people who don't know each other for the profit of people who know each other but don't massacre each other.
—Paul Valery

AT ONE POINT, I learned Jasmina was staying with her aunt in the neighborhood called Bistrik, close to Vratnik. I headed there one day, by myself, to find her. I knocked on the door and was greeted by her cousin Amela, whom I remembered as a cheerful young lady with luscious dark hair, full lips, and enormous eyes. When she opened the door, she looked as if a ghost took over her body. She looked serious, no smile to greet me. Before the war, Amela and her older brother had a Doberman, but the dog either died during the war or they got rid of him. Behind Amela stood Jasmina. I exclaimed in happiness and lifted my arms as if to give her a big hug, but Jasmina seemed somewhat lifeless, as if she wasn't pleased I was there.

This new response from her confused me. She was my best friend, and I thought she'd be happy to see me. For a second, I thought that perhaps I had done something that would have made her resentful or angry with me. Perhaps she didn't like that I escaped the morning massacre in our neighborhood on June 17. Perhaps she might have thought I felt I was better than her now that I didn't experience the atrocities, fear, and confusion that morning. But all of that was in my head. Survivor's guilt. They asked me to come in and Jasmina announced she'd get ready and we would take a walk downtown. She had a few cigarettes, and she was still hiding from her family that she smoked.

Jasmina had changed profoundly. She lost a spark, her sense of humor, and the smile that was always on her cute face. We walked around downtown to catch up, talking about things that had happened since we last saw each other. Last time I saw her was half a year ago, in April, when Amra and I last showed up for lunch at Aerdromsko Naselje and then headed back to Munevera's and Keko's place. As we walked through familiar streets, we were looking for a place to light a cigarette and finally have a face-to-face conversation.

Hotel Europe was one of the oldest hotels in Sarajevo. It was built in the nineteenth century and stood near the bazaar built during the Ottoman Empire. Hotel Europe was the place my parents first met in the seventies during a New Year's Eve celebration. My dad spotted my mother in the crowd, and when he mustered up the courage, he approached and asked her to dance.

The hotel looked different that day. All the windows were smashed, and inside on the ground floor, where the foyer and a bar used to be, was now destroyed and looted space. We entered through a glassless window and spotted a couple of chairs in a corner, looking damp and dirty, but we didn't let that bother us like it might have before. Jasmina gave me a cigarette as we sat down. We both enjoyed inhaling and exhaling smoke as if we had just been reunited with a higher spirit.

"So, how's everything going?" I asked. She shrugged, exhaled the smoke, and dropped her eyes down.

"I haven't recovered from that morning yet. It was brutal."

"I really want to hear what happened that morning. If you don't mind." I knew that recollecting the events from June 17 would bring the pain back again.

"It all seemed so surreal. We woke up sometime around five o'clock, and we heard our neighbors saying that tanks were coming from different sides of the neighborhood. My mom, Jasmin, and I—it all happened fast—got out of the house and escaped somehow. Our neighbors told us it was too risky, but we ignored them." She flicked the ash of her cigarette to the bare ground. "We crossed the street and got to the other side of the building and then walked along the building, trying to find a safe place. We heard the rumblings on the streets, people screaming, and tanks' engines get-ting closer and closer. I will never forget the voices of these soldiers shouting out and calling people to get out of their homes."

My eyes were wide open, anticipating the rest of the story. I was trying to imagine the fear of being discovered, the fear of being slaughtered right on the spot because you were trying to escape death, the fear of getting into the hands of monsters who might rape, torture, and discard you later.

"And so we kept running along the buildings, and suddenly I felt I was bleeding. My period wasn't due yet, but I felt that warm sensation. The people's voices were horrific. It sounded chaotic, but we didn't get distracted and kept toward the safe zone. I can't tell how long it took us, but we finally arrived in Dobrinja, leaving the neighborhood behind. I just couldn't believe that we had escaped. It was a miracle."

"That sounds horrible." I wanted to tell her about my own experiences of living in Dobrinja Five and not being able to leave the house for months. Or how I saw my uncle Ramiz dying in front of my eyes. But I kept quiet and listened to what she had to say.

Our gathering was disappointing. It made me feel as if I was a lesser victim, a pair of ears that needed to listen. But I learned something new. I learned you could escape from terror only if you got lucky, and no other way.

It also made me realize that my life started anew. New people came to my life while people I knew all my life were profoundly changing and would never be the same. I also had a new home. New neighbors. New points of view. New everything. It was the perfect divide between peace and war, a marker that clearly set a difference between then and now.

I made trips downtown at least two to three times a week, but I wasn't going out of my way to see Jasmina again. Aida and I continued to be the primary water fetchers. Our role was serious, and the whole family depended on our efforts. In the beginning, Aida made fun of me because I was weak and I couldn't push the wheelbarrow, but after a month, I could finally keep up with her.

Sarajevo Klas, the bread factory, produced limited amounts of bread during the war. The only way to buy bread was to get up at four thirty in the morning and arrive shortly after the curfew at five and wait in long lines. Since the daily allowance was one loaf per person, Aida and I would both clock in to buy one each. One morning, bread was sold out just as it was our turn in line. That didn't discourage us from getting up early and go again. We took it as our job. We also volunteered at Sumeja, but Aida got accused of stealing a couple of brown packages, which I later learned she had, so we were both let go. Our volunteering ended immediately thereafter.

When we smoked, we hid under the stairway that led to the second floor of the house. It was getting dark one day, and Aida and I left the apartment, telling everyone we'd be right back. Just as we lit our cigarette, we heard steps coming our way. Before we could extinguish the cigarette, my uncle's colossal figure appeared before our eyes, and he instantly grabbed Aida and beat her with his bare hands. He hit her all over her body while she was hysterically crying. He screamed at her with his raspy voice, straining to get louder. I just stood there, frozen, watching the entire scene.

"There's nothing I can do to you,"—he pointed his finger at me —"but I'm going to tell Azra you smoke as soon as I talk to her."

My blood froze, and now I had another concern to live with. My mother. She was a tough cookie, but I had hoped maybe the war had softened her up a bit. I never found out what her reaction would be because my uncle never told her.

Growing up as siblings in the same family of seven kids, my uncle and my mother were similar in raising their own children. They had the same morals and similar expectations as us. We feared them more than anything in the world.

When winter came, we moved to the first floor, as the basement was too moldy and cold. Both households had a wood stove, so it was more convenient to live there. Aida and I slept on the floor of Grandmother's living room while Grandmother slept on the sofa along the windows. She was so quiet in her sleep that sometimes we wondered if she might have passed away. We'd call her, "Nano, nano," but she would stay quiet. We had to be silent in order to hear her breathing and be reassured she was still alive.

At some point, Aida and I got desperate for cigarettes. We knew some people who smoked, but cigarettes were difficult to come by during the war. Aida had discovered that Grandmother had an old pack of cigarettes in her chest in the bedroom. She whispered about this discovery to me one night, and we stuck out of bed and tiptoed through the hallway to the bedroom. As the house was old and the floor made of wood, the floor screeched beneath our feet, making us afraid we'd wake up Grandmother. When we entered the room, the moon shone brightly and we could see everything clearly. We opened up the chest door and took the pack of cigarettes. It was one of the oldest packs I had ever seen in my life. It must have been at least twenty years old, and even the brand, Lara, no longer existed. The orange package was open, missing only a few cigarettes. The cigarettes were extremely dry, and when we finally smoked them, we realized the age from the burning in our lungs. During our hunt for cigarettes, we also discovered cookies in the chest. We took those as well and ate them all in one sitting. A couple of days later, Grandmother discovered the cookies were gone. She told everybody. Grandmother yelled at us, because she couldn't believe we had the nerve to steal from her. Sabaheta was pouting all day long, and she was angry because we didn't share the cookies and also because Grandmother never mentioned them. In all the confrontation within the family, and the war scarcity and mayhem, Aida and I found it amusing and satisfying that we had eaten cookies.

CHAPTER 9

Vegetables

*A*ll wars are follies, very expensive and very mischievous ones.
  —Benjamin Franklin

SINCE THE BEGINNING of the war, we had eaten no fresh meat, eggs, milk, fruit, or vegetables. The food we received as humanitarian aid was powdered and processed. Aida knew that some of Grandmother's neighbors grew vegetables in their yard. She plotted a way to get a hold of those vegetables and create an opportunity for the family to enjoy them. Aida knew exactly whose neighbors' gardens to visit.

"But I've stolen nothing in my life. I'm not sure I want to do this," I told her.

"But there are so many vegetables—enough to feed everyone in the neighborhood, believe me."

"Yeah, but we can't just go to someone's backyard and take their vegetables."

"Why not? Our second door neighbor is kinda mean. She deserves this. And the old man behind the corner, well, he's kinda old. He will never notice the missing vegetables." Any justification she could think of worked at that moment.

"Okay, but if we get caught, we will be in big trouble," I said.

"No one is gonna catch us. You're just paranoid." She giggled. One night, when Grandmother slept soundly, Aida and I embarked on another journey of thievery, this time in the neighbors' yards. Since all the neighbors knew each other and the curfew was in full swing, we put our pajama tops on our heads so no one could recognize us if they caught us. Both she and I were tomboys when we were younger, so climbing fences and walls was a piece of cake.

A few days earlier, I pulled a prank on Aida before we headed out to buy bread. I'd climb the front yard gate that was locked in the evening for safety and I would hide somewhere on the other side of the gate so she would hopefully end up looking for me around the house and, after being unable to find me, wonder where the heck I was. She had the key to the gate and was going to unlock it for us. I placed my right foot carefully on the first bar across the gate, then placed my left foot on the second bar, way up high, and then put my first leg across the gate, landing the foot on the bar on the other side. Then I placed my left foot on the bar and was ready to jump. But when I jumped, the back of my jacket caught on the top of a vertical bar, and suddenly my feet were dangling as if someone hung me on a hook. I tried hard to free myself. I desperately reached for my jacket to move it off the bar, but I couldn't. I moved my feet around, hoping to get them on the bars now sitting behind me, prop myself up, and free the jacket, but to no avail.

Sabaheta showed up, as she was heading to the Sarajevo hospital where she resumed work part time. She unlocked the gate door, turned to me, and asked, "What are you doing up there?" Before I could explain how I got stuck, she walked away. For a second, I thought to myself that if a shell fell on the street, I'd probably be dead. Just like that. The thought of being dead from sheer stupidity made me nervous. As my thoughts about a shell falling near me raced, the kicking of my feet made me look more and more like a wild animal caught in a cage. Two people walked by but didn't even seem to pay attention, as if I wasn't even there.

Five minutes later, Aida showed up, and as soon as she saw me, she burst into uncontrollable laughter.

"Stop laughing, you dork, and get me off. Get...me...off!" I pleaded with her, as I was feeling uncomfortable. When she finally composed herself, she pulled my jacket off the bar, and I jumped to freedom. Obviously, my plan to hide from Aida did not work.

The previous gate climbing experience didn't discourage me from continuing with our plan. We stole out of bed and climbed the nine-foot-high front gate until we reached the street on the other side.

We tiptoed down the street, hoping not to run into soldiers or wake up the neighborhood void of any sounds. The moon was bright, and our surroundings were clear as daylight. We heard bullets fired in a distance, but it did not deter us from going forward. We arrived at the first garden and climbed over a fence, behind which we saw a miracle of plentiful vegetables sitting on the ground. I stood there for a few seconds in disbelief, since the growing vegetables seemed like a dream.

"Let's go. Why are you standing there and staring?" Aida rushed me.

We picked some tomatoes, zucchinis, and pumpkins and placed them in our pajama tops, holding it close with hands so as not to lose the vegetables on our way home. When we returned to the house, we climbed up the gate again and strolled inside. We put all the vegetables in the kitchen sink and went back to bed. Pumped from the adrenaline, we couldn't stay still in bed, so we went for round two shortly thereafter. We visited a couple of different gardens and gathered a few more tomatoes.

When Grandmother walked into the kitchen in the morning, she let out a long "ah", disbelieving what she saw. She came out of the pantry, came to the room, paused for a second, and went back to the pantry again. We watched a shocking grimace form on her face while Aida and I smiled, pleased at Grandmother's reaction. We thought we scored a prize in her eyes. Instead, she began to scream and yell, "What have you done? Neighbors will find out, and you will be in big trouble! How dare you go out there and steal? Shame on you. Shame on you!" Grandmother was livid all day long. Later in the day, Aunt Sabaheta tried to calm her down while her sons were holding a tomato in their hands before taking a bite.

"Relax, Mother. No one is going to find out."

I ate only half a tomato of all the things we had taken. The following day, I confessed in my diary:

> This was a battle for survival because every single human being attempts to survive. We didn't steal for the sake of a childish game, but for the sake of the lack of food in our house—so that we could have something to eat. Yes, this is called a battle for survival. God will forgive my sin, and I still believe in the old saying "Help yourself, and God will help you."

Sarajevo, October 12, 1992.

BUT MY GRANDMOTHER didn't think so. She was fed up with us, so she told us we could no longer sleep at her place. We moved to the second floor as opposed to the basement. Aida and I slept in her old room that faced the neighbors' houses. The room next to hers became inhabitable when a shell broke all the windows and damaged the roof above at the beginning of the war.

At night, it was extremely quiet, with a few bullet shots heard from afar. Since there was no longer light pollution in the city, we clearly saw stars and watched them while sitting on the windowsill at night. Despite the incident of being caught smoking, we hadn't quit. With the winter underway, colder nights kept us awake. I wore a couple of pajama tops and a heavy sweater, and we covered ourselves with several blankets to keep warm. Since we could no longer feel the difference between the inside and outside temperature, we kept the window open and smoked at the window.

One particular evening, we noticed my uncle didn't return home from his civic duties. We weren't completely sure; it was possible we didn't hear him walk through the door, or perhaps he was downstairs at Grandmother's place. In the early morning, around six o'clock, we heard the front door open and slam. We discovered my uncle standing in the hallway, covered in dry mud, looking exhausted. He didn't want to talk to us and went straight to bed. When he woke up, he told us that the Bosnian Army assigned him and other men to dig trenches on nearby hills. He tried to get out of it, based on his health conditions, but to no avail. Instead, he dug a trench all night. Aida and I went back to her room and cried like babies.

Aida and I went downtown the following day for our usual domestic duties, and on our way home, we stopped by an Orthodox church. I had never been to a church and knew little about what activities took place, but I knew the obvious that one could pray. Inside, the church was dark, and in one corner stood what seemed to be a coffin. The church was tiny, comprising two rooms and made of stonewalls. The church had already had visitors earlier, with a few lit candles sitting among the unlit ones. We bought a couple of candles and positioned where all the other candles sat. When we lit them, we told each other that we dedicated it to Uncle Hamo. We whispered a few prayers to ourselves. I said something I had made up right there and then. I felt it deep down. Maybe this could work. Maybe it would save him. Save us.

After the incident with my uncle, we developed a new appreciation for both him and his wife. Aida and I took the initiative of learning how to cook. We realized it wasn't fair to have Šefika cook for us all the time. We learned how to make a Bosnian pie and stretch dough. It was my first time cooking savory food, but the war definitely wasn't quite the right time to learn well.

In all the mayhem, I developed a desire to become a journalist. And so did Aida. We daydreamed about living in London and Paris and naively plotted ways to get on a convoy from Sarajevo to a safe zone and find our way to one of those cities.

"Maybe we can talk to the UN soldiers and convince them to hide us in their vehicles and get us out of Sarajevo," one of us joked. Throughout the city were UN tanks whose purpose we often questioned. They were observers, someone said. Observing wasn't what the citizens quite needed during the war.

"Nah, they are useless," we concluded.

We began writing journal entries and shared them with Sabaheta and the cousins. Aida was superior in her writing skills, and so I was hesitant to share mine, even though it was well received. We wrote in the notebooks Aida used for her physics and German classes in high school. She no longer needed them. We resolved to write a letter to an imaginary friend, describing the current circumstances, and I wrote:

A Letter to a Former Friend

Here, my friend, while I am sitting in a cold room in front of a candle and a slice of dry bread, I am trying to finish writing you this letter. Probably so you remember me once again. Friend, I wish you were here, next to me, to feel at least one day of the war, to hear a sound of a zooming shell, or at least to feel hunger. Mainly, I want to tell you that it isn't easy to watch the death ruins, tragedy that happens all around me. Friend, would you help me if I told you there was no bread in my house, water, or even a small consolation? I wish I were in London, Paris, or Vienna right now to listen to the songs of youth rather than those of war and patriotism, or not to watch young boys in uniforms and garbage all over the streets. My friend, do you know that I am hungry for an apple, a pear while you're indulging tropic fruits and cocktails under a palm tree or in a shadow of a pine tree. It doesn't matter where, but at least you don't feel the same desire for pleasure and the need for optimism like I do. And my optimism has vanished... Did all of this have to happen? Does a difference between you and me have to exist? You were born in this city, like me, yet you are not here, next to me. But you could've said a few words before you left: "There will be war," you could've said. "Come with me" or "Take good care," but you, my friend, just disappeared, I am hoping, forever.

I know I will never see you again, never tell you about the death of my uncle, never describe you a blast of a shell on the street, so here is this letter probably so you remember me once again. Farewell, my former friend. If I vanish, tell everyone that I died with the heart full of patriotism and that I always lived for this city.

Sarajevo, December 5, 1992

CHAPTER 10

The Visit

*W*ar is not an adventure. It is a disease. It is like typhus.
—Antoine de Saint-Exupery

WITH DECEMBER'S ARRIVAL, the cold had clearly set its mark on the city. Aida and I continued to bring water uphill and get up early in the morning to buy bread. I missed my immediate family more than ever, and I didn't know when I was going to see them again. My uncle Muhamed and aunt Šefika took care of me as if I was their own child, but I still yearned for my true family and all the little habits we had developed during the war, like playing solitaire, drawing faces, or playing guitar and singing all night.

At the end of December, on a typical war day, we were all sitting in our grandmother's living room when suddenly, the front gate's door screeched. We looked through the window and saw Amra and Anis walk through the gate door. We all immediately jumped up to go greet them. My grandmother cried, and she immediately peed herself, whether out of joy or sadness, when she saw Amra. Amra was one of her favorite grandchildren. When our grandfather was alive and Amra was around one-year-old, he'd carry ice cream for Amra from a few blocks away while the ice cream was melting down his hand. Amra had a calm personality. She was always quiet, and she had the biggest baby cheeks everyone would notice and comment.

No one expected them to visit. The true nature of the war was living through many surprises, including this joyful one. I was so happy Amra and Anis came to visit that I immediately resolved to go back to Dobrinja with them.

"Are you sure?" Amra said.

"Yes, I am sure. A hundred percent." I spoke with confidence. Aida cried.

"Please don't leave me. Please, please, please."

"The conditions are just as you left them, you know," Amra retorted.

"I don't care." I had no feelings about this, and I had no empathy for Aida.

"Suit yourself, but when you come back, you know it will be the same." Amra tried. "Plus, it's been freezing in the house."

"Whatever. I'm used to it."

No one could order me around. I was a water fetcher, a bread buyer, a vegetable procurer, and a newly fashioned cook. I was a war-matured adolescent, taking care of my family and myself. I could decide on my own. No one could tell me what to do any longer. But Amra realized how nice it was to be walking on the streets of Sarajevo. She would have perhaps stayed at Grandmother's, but Anis was her anchor in Dobrinja—she would never desert him under any circumstances.

The following day, we left Vratnik on foot, as we didn't have organized transportation. We said our goodbyes, with Aida tearful and sad for my departure. She lost her partner in crime. If stealing was a true crime, I no longer wanted to be her partner.

Uncle Hamo gave us a small woodstove to take back home. The

stove was made of an old hospital sterilizer, to which metal legs and a chimney pipe were attached, and the entire stove was painted silver. My family in Dobrinja still struggled with heating the house, and they used the next-door neighbor's stove to cook. Anis carried the stove on his back until we got to the main street and hitchhiked from Vratnik to Dobrinja. We didn't see too many vehicles on the road because fuel was scarce, so we waited and waited until one finally stopped for us.

As we approached Dobrinja, gunshots became louder and more frequent. On the border between Dobrinja and Mojmilo stood a waiting station where people, mostly civilians, looked for a vehicle to pick them up and take them to Dobrinja. The distance between the waiting station and our home building was only a ten-minute walk, but that walk could be deadly. After nearly an hour, a random driver picked us up, and we finally arrived home safe. When my mother opened the door, she had a huge smile on her face and gave me a big hug and kisses. She was just as happy seeing the stove as she knew it would make our lives easier.

The days following my arrival, I shared my experiences living in Vratnik with my family. We would sit around the living room table, look at one another through the flickering lights of the *kandilo*, and laugh at my stories. I told them about how I got stuck, hanging on the gate, and how Grandmother got upset when we stole vegetables. I impersonated Uncle Muhamed, complaining about soup, or any other story I thought would make my mother laugh. It was good to be home. Vratnik was a key to freedom, but Dobrinja was a key to freedom to be more myself in the comfort of my family.

CHAPTER 11

Prayer

*W*ar is a defeat for humanity.
  —Pope John Paul II

WE INSTALLED our new woodstove in a corner of the dining room, and the walls were quickly turning dark from the smoke. At night, we couldn't see all the dirt in the house, but during the day, it was apparent that the walls and the rest of the house were unmanageable. It was already January 1993, and the winter was brutally cold. The pipes in the basement often froze, making it difficult for us to get water. The army in Dobrinja Five dug out a well near the garage where people ventured out when the Serbs took a break from shooting at us. My mother didn't allow Amra and me to go, as the mortality rate in Dobrinja remained high and random killings common. This differed from my experience in Vratnik, and it was hard to get used to the old ways.

While I lived in Vratnik, the Army handed Anis an apartment in our building in a neighboring subdivision. He was entitled to it as a soldier. A lot of apartments stayed empty, as many owners fled at the beginning of the war. The apartment was on the ground floor, tucked in a corner, facing the neighborhood on one side and the garage on the other. Even though he had his own apartment, from the very beginning, he was spending most of his time in our apartment, and my mom took him in as her own son. She cooked for him, she washed his clothes, and she even became affectionate to him. Anis's family lived in Brčko before the war, a city in the northern part of Bosnia, close to the Croatian border. In the beginning of the war, his parents and his sister fled to Germany and got menial jobs as refugees.

Right from the beginning, Anis would tease me and made fun of me in front of my family. His teasing became more intense after my return from Vratnik. My parents and Amra thought it was out of affection, but I didn't find it either amusing or affectionate at all. I had always been a sensitive kid—one that was bullied by classmates and made fun of most of her elementary school life. Anis teased me one night after we went to bed, and I recounted my experiences in Vratnik. I was so fed up, I cried. My father defended me and raised his voice, telling him to stop. Anis began yelling back, and their words fired back and forth at each other. Anis grabbed a porcelain mug and smashed it against the floor. I jumped immediately and felt scared that he might have wanted to hurt us. Growing up, I hadn't experienced physical violence between my parents or Amra. My parents often communicated by screaming and yelling, but no one ever broke anything because of anger.

My father told him to leave our house immediately. So he did. He went to his apartment downstairs. My mother felt terrible for him because he had no way to heat the space, so he was guaranteed to be cold. Amra was just as shocked as everyone else.

When the dust settled, Amra went to visit Anis at his apartment a couple of days later, and everything was more or less back to normal. He apologized to everyone, but the image and sound of the mug breaking was still echoing in my mind.

The winter stubbornly continued to be cold. January passed uneventfully. I missed my trips downtown with Aida and regretted returning to Dobrinja. February 23 came, marking the first day of Ramadan. Except for my grandmothers and older relatives, no one else in our family was religious. Growing up in the former Yugoslavia, religion was frowned upon, as the communist party didn't allow anyone to practice openly. For the same reason, my parents never went to a mosque, and neither did Amra and I. My grandmother, when we stayed over at her place when we were kids, had taught us a couple of prayers, which she whispered every night in bed. I didn't know what they meant in Arabic, but they were simple enough to memorize. On both sides of the family, Eid, a Muslim holiday, was celebrated, but it was more of a cultural gesture than a religious one. With the war raging throughout the country, many people in Bosnia turned to religion, and as a result, a lot of mosques were being established in basements. A mosque opened up in the building across from us so people could have easy access to a shrine.

Munevera was brave enough to visit us one day, and she announced she was going to fast during Ramadan. I gave it some thought myself and decided I would, too, even though I had never done it in my life. Fasting during Ramadan could be an intense experience, as a person isn't allowed to eat and drink or smoke from dawn to dusk.

I was hungry most of the time anyway, so fasting would be easy. With shorter days in the winter, I figured fasting might be easier to manage. While at it, I decided it would be best to pray five times a day to make my fasting worthwhile. But my biggest problem was not knowing one prayer. Even the one my grandmother taught us, I didn't know what it was or what it meant. In fact, all my life, I had never set foot in a mosque even though Sarajevo had dozens. Munevera found a way to send me a book with prayers. On the left side of the page, they were written in Arabic; on the other side, they were written in Bosnian, with correct pronunciation. It was like a little Muslim prayer book for dummies.

I taught myself how to pray five times a day. I would first figure out what direction Mecca was in so I could face that way. I'd wash my face, my feet, and my hands and cover my head so my hair didn't show. The neighborhood mosque gave out handouts for the prayer times on each day during Ramadan. Typically, in peacetime, a muezzin from a mosque minaret would call for a time for prayer, or a recording would play, but not during the war. When the time for a prayer came, I would put a towel on the floor, the dummies book right next to it, and then began by whispering prayers in the standing position. When I bent down to the ground, I'd peek at the book with a corner of my eye just to make sure I had missed no words or phrases.

Once the darkness came and the fasting concluded, I attended to a feast my mother made for me. I began going to the mosque every night right after the feast. The army kitchen began making *somun*—a circled and fluffy bread popular during Ramadan. Whoever went to the mosque would get one or two. Amra was so excited about eating the *somun* that every evening, she waited for me at the door with a huge smile on her face. By day five, I felt gratified by the entire experience. Shells could drop around me, mugs could break, people could be mean, but I remained calm and centered. I felt some force inside me that kept me hopeful and somehow connected to a higher power.

Around this time, several battles to take back the Bosnian land were happening in and around the city. The army in Dobrinja Five began recruiting many soldiers to be sent to Mount Igman, where the most frightful and fierce battles took place. Anis came home one day and announced they had chosen him and he'd leave a couple of days later. Amra cried both days, and so did my mother. Amra and Anis spent a lot of time at Anis's apartment downstairs as if they were having a long farewell party. A lot of the soldiers who had already been sent to that battle area had lost their lives.

I had heard one time that a prayer made wishes come true, but I never believed it. It was an old wives' tale. Though still skeptical, just before my usual daily prayer, I wished Anis didn't go to battle. I felt a thousand little sunrays were beaming at me when I spoke the wish words in my mind.

The wish was a joke. Anis was still getting ready, and his departure became certain when he packed his large army backpack, layers of clothes, and some food for the road. He came upstairs to say good-byes, a gun on his shoulder, the heavy backpack, a green uniform on his slim body, and the boots that looked two sizes too big. We hugged and kissed him and wished him luck. Amra was hyperventilating, covered in tears. The sad look on his face almost made me believe that he, too, was immensely scared. He might never return. No one knew how long the battle would last or when Anis would return home. After he finally left, we went about our own business as usual. The space felt somewhat empty, like a piece of comfortable furniture was suddenly missing.

A few hours later, someone knocked on our door. We all looked at each other and asked, "Who the heck is this now?" When my mom opened the door, Anis was standing right there.

"Ahhhhh. It's Anis!" Amra jumped out of her seat. "What are you doing here?" my mom happily asked.

"They told me they don't need me, so they sent me back home."

"Really? Did they give you a reason?" someone said.

"No, not really." He shrugged his shoulders. "They just told me to go back home."

I couldn't believe what had just happened. Whether it was a coincidence or the true power of the prayer, Anis's return home was a miracle. After so many recent losses, I was convinced someone or something wanted to make me smile at last. I continued to pray, fast, and be more involved in the mosque activities. I decided I would be in a mosque choir, singing religious songs in Arabic. The one time I attempted to sing, mumbling words and pretending I knew the song inside and out, the young imam looked at me and laughed.

"You didn't memorize the lyrics well, did you?"

I said nothing in return. I just looked down and blushed. So much for trying! I never wanted to go to the mosque again. And I didn't. My religious life was short-lived. To this day, it remains to be the only one.

CHAPTER 12

Schoolmates

War grows out of the desire of the individual to gain advantage at the expense of his fellow man.
—Napoleon Hill

AT THE END of March in 1993, I turned fifteen. Rumors circled around Dobrinja that schools were opening soon. I was wondering how and where, since the Serbs still shelled us at unpredictable times and people were still dying on the streets of Dobrinja. Around April, parents were being told that all schooling would take place in the basements of our buildings, and teachers would come to the students. This way, they would keep children safe from danger. It had been more than a year since I went to school at that point. I was in the eighth grade when the war began, the last grade of elementary school. Since we were close to finishing the grade at the brink of the war, they decided children would resume schooling into the next grade.

For me, that meant I would be in ninth grade, the first year in high school.

I was ready for new beginnings. My classmates would be new to me, and no one would know I was subject to bullying and name-calling in the past. I was looking forward to making new friends and starting my school life anew. How many children lived in Dobrinja Five? I was clueless. Aside from the youth club that was short-lived, there wasn't a place to meet or make acquaintances with people of similar ages, backgrounds, or interests. At least now everyone had the same background of living through the war and the only interest in survival. Since almost all the high schools throughout Sarajevo were physically located outside of Dobrinja, these high schools were reestablished on a smaller scale with the empty spaces in our buildings repurposed for classes. Before the war, Amra was enrolled in the applied arts high school, and she learned that her new school would be in Dobrinja Three, across the Dobrinja stream. She would have to go as often as possible, but if danger became imminent, her absence would be excused. In the meantime, Amra volunteered to teach art classes to first graders in the basement across the street. She had to report every other day to teach, which eventually turned into babysitting. Ever since Uncle Ramiz was killed on the street, and Sabaheta's fear and sorrow had a lot to do with it, Amra was so frightened to walk outside, even for short distances, that she soon quit thereafter. When she went to school across the stream, Anis would accompany her to school and pick her up after classes.

A new high school was established—Gimnazija Dobrinja—where I had enrolled. I learned shortly after that my classes would be held in the basement of our subdivision. They had cleaned a room in the basement and put old desks and chairs inside. The windows were covered halfway with sandbags for protection. Natural light could beam in and help us see each other and read. The teachers were diligent in showing up from different parts of Dobrinja and brought single paper sheets on which lessons were typed out. We didn't learn from any textbooks or write in notebooks; I didn't even bring a pen or a pencil on my first day. The lessons were minimal, but they became our alternative sources of knowledge and learning, and this was the best the teachers could do.

On the first day of school, I met my classmates. The young man I was once fascinated with, Faruk, was in my class. I was too shy to talk to him, even though he was friendly and goofy. When I saw him up close, I examined his facial features more carefully, and no longer found him attractive. Suddenly, my fascination with him was gone. A girl named Enisa with bright red cheeks and a joyful demeanor sat in the first row and asked a lot of questions. I thought she was exceptionally smart and friendly. She lived in the subdivision next to Emir's and had a big crush on him, but the feeling was not mutual.

And then there was Selma. Selma was a short girl who had black hair to her shoulders and wore thick prescription glasses over her dark brown eyes. Selma had a fierce personality. When she spoke, her voice sounded mature, and her laughter loud and confident. I soon learned that she was an only child, and her parents probably gave her much attention to be a fun, free spirit. To my surprise, she and I connected right away. She lived in a building across from mine, on the ground floor. She had running water in her house, and I envied her she didn't have to go to the basement to fetch water all the time. Over time, I learned Selma used the school as her playground. She'd make fun of our young history teacher, Smajo, and when I noticed that he was overly amused and happy to hear her merriment, I joined in. This was not typical of me. In peacetime, I feared authority. At home and in school, we were taught to respect our parents, our teachers, our elders, and government-associated parties. I was one of those children who wanted to impress teachers and be helpful to them.

When I was in the first grade, my mother discovered a plastic bag in the back pocket of my jeans and asked me what the bag was doing there. Frequently, my teacher had asked the students if they had a plastic bag, and no one had one.

"What do you need the plastic bag for?" asked my mom.

"If the teacher needs one, I want to give it to her." My mother laughed at me.

You could try to show disrespect, but it wouldn't end well. When

Selma, and then I, made fun of Smajo, he would begin to laugh and say, "Look at this girl Selma. And Nadija. You are both so clueless. I am going to fail both of you."

"You? You look like you don't know how to eat bread." I was going straight to hell, I was sure. But he laughed at our jokes and ended up giving us satisfactory grades.

My network of schoolmates grew rapidly as high school ramped up. Selma told me that a boy our age named Igor lived in her building subdivision. His mother was widowed and he had a younger sister. He was a Christian, from a mixed marriage, his mother being an Orthodox and father a Catholic. She wanted to set me up with him because he had seen me recently and told Selma that he wanted to get to know me better. I met him once, playing billiards in one of the former stores near the old Red Cross office. The neighboring children made fun of him when they saw his hair and suggested that he have a hair operation. His hair was long, down the middle, and greasy, as if he washed it with oil. The Muslim teenagers felt no remorse for people like Igor, a suspicious Christian, and they'd target him and subject him to bullying, out of sheer frustration and rage at everything that was happening. He laughed at their snarks and handled all so calmly, which I found admirable.

One day, Selma arranged for the two of us to meet in the garage right after school. Selma gave him all the details of what time the last class was over. I wasn't sure that I wanted to do it, because I didn't think my parents would appreciate their daughter dating a Christian boy. When we were growing up, our grandmother and parents would beat it in our heads to marry one of our own—an educated Muslim boy born in Sarajevo, who grew up in a family of decency and similar values. But my desire to connect with boys grew proportionately with my age, and at fifteen, I finally wanted to experience a girl-boy relationship and see for myself how that felt. When I arrived, I saw him up close for the first time. He looked different at a closer distance—his oily hair split down the middle didn't suit his long and freckled face.

After a round of awkward introductions, Igor tried to kiss me several times, but I pulled away every time. When I was twelve, Aida, Amra, and I habitually went to a disco every Saturday at Hotel Europe in downtown Sarajevo. We would go to our grandmother's in the morning, and then the three of us would get ready to go dancing. We'd wear short tight dresses and put makeup on, hoping to look hip and attract boys, just for fun. The disco for children our age began at 5:00 p.m. and went on until about 8:00 p.m. On one of those occasions, I had met a boy, quite tall, with short spiky hair, someone I found unattractive, who asked me to take a walk to the nearby park with him. I had agreed, because the opportunity to be alone with a boy finally knocked on my door. He took me by the hand and led me to a bench. Being too shy, I had avoided chances of being alone with a boy or try to kiss. I lived through romantic relationships vicariously through Amra, who had a first boyfriend in her early teens. At the same age, I had barely spoken to boys. But I was willing to change that —to give myself a chance to not be so estranged from romance and perhaps follow Amra's footsteps. She was an older sister, after all, and perhaps my role model. He sat down and pulled me to sit on his lap. Then he brought his face closer to mine and began French kissing me. I stuck out my tongue and tried to swirl it around, hoping I would nail it immediately. Suddenly, he pushed me away and said, "You don't know how to French kiss, do you?"

I didn't know what to say. I immediately stood up. He did the same and walked away without saying a word. I felt humiliated and embarrassed. The experience had left a mark on me. Now I didn't want to kiss Igor in order to save myself from more embarrassment.

He'd still invite me to his place, and we hung out in his room while he played his guitar. He would hold me in his arms, play with my hair, talk to me about different things, and do his best to make me laugh. On my way home one day, we went to his living room to talk to his mother. We began discussing what was going on around the neighborhood, all the battles that took place, all the neighbors who were killed recently.

And then she said, "Our army was shooting toward the building when I was on the balcony, and I had to run inside as fast as possible."

When she said, "Our army," however, she pointed at the Serbian village. Was there some kind of confusion? Did she consider the Serbs our army? Did she know I was Muslim? I wasn't sure I heard it correctly, but when I turned to Igor, his eyes looked as big as a house. He interrupted his mother and ushered me to the hallway, where we said goodbyes.

After my visit, Igor refused to hang out with me again. We would say hi to each other, but he never really gave me the explanation why he broke up with me. I thought maybe he was fed up with the fact I didn't want to kiss him. Or maybe he didn't want me to risk my life by running under imminent shells to come to his place to hang out.

Several weeks later, Igor, his mother, and his sister disappeared. We didn't know where they went or how. But we speculated that they probably had crossed over to the Serbian village. When I learned he was gone, I almost wished he had broken up with me for the reasons I had thought. I felt betrayed by his disappearance even though I had invested little in our friendship.

CHAPTER 13

The Barbershop

*A*n unjust peace is better than a just war.
    —Marcus Tullius Cicero

SCHOOL EITHER WAS GOING WELL MOSTLY or not at all, mainly because such were the circumstances. Neither the teachers nor the students took it too seriously. After the teachers gave us our single sheet lessons, they would set a date to return to the basement in order for us to take either an oral or written exam. When the shooting was intense, we would sit in the basement for as long as necessary and wait for the teacher to arrive. If after twenty minutes the teacher didn't show, it was clear he or she wouldn't show at all.

Dobrinja continued to breed danger daily. On June 1, 1993, while playing soccer on a field hidden from the enemy, a shell burst on the field and killed several young boys during their game. We stood on the balcony, watching the ambulance rush downtown with legs and feet lifelessly dangling from the back. When serious injuries resulted from the shelling, the injured were taken to the Sarajevo downtown hospital, as the Dobrinja hospital didn't have the means to care for them. After this incident, we'd be weary and not go outside for a couple of days. Shortly after, we'd pretend to have recovered and carry on with our lives.

Amra's high school was in Dobrinja Three, a few blocks from our building. It was located across the bridge from where Keko and Munevera lived. She didn't have to attend her classes as often as I, but when she did, Anis would accompany her as if he was her personal bodyguard. One day, the two of them came home in cuts and bruises. Apparently, darkness had already wrapped up the neighborhood when they left the school, and instead of taking an immediate left, they kept going straight, only to end up falling in a hole about two feet deep. The streetlights in Sarajevo were out, making nights exceptionally dark, and even more so with overhanging clouds.

Selma once told me she worked as an apprentice in a barbershop next to the former Red Cross. Amazingly, the barbershop was a barbershop before the war. The windows were all broken, like any other store along the strip, but the barbershop was protected by sandbags from top to bottom. The electricity was supplied by a generator and, by some strange luck, would pump water through the faucet. Huso was one of the best barbers in Sarajevo and Selma's father's good friend.

I went to visit Selma at the barbershop one day. I watched her slowly cut a young boy's hair while Huso would advise her how to hold the comb and scissors and tell her where to snip more, where less. She had started off with experimenting on children, as most of Huso's clientele were soldiers who were always either too tired for a slow haircut session or were in a rush to sentry duty. Children had more time on their hands, and their parents could tolerate a mediocre haircut. Selma was slow at first, cutting and snipping to the best of her abilities. When she finished her experiment, Huso would take over and properly fix the haircut.

Huso had a dry sense of humor. For a barber, he had a horrible haircut that looked as if he was electrocuted. He was married with two small children. He worked extremely hard as a barber to ensure that he would not be enlisted in the Army as a soldier. He was recruited as the army barber, because he was the only barber in the neighborhood. The barbershop was never empty. Soldiers had priority, whereas civilians could come only at a certain time window. The business was growing fierce, and Huso needed more help to keep up with the demand of his job.

One day, when I came over for a visit, he approached me with a broom and stuck it out. "Here, you want to help?"

I stood up right away, grabbed the broom, and began sweeping the hair spread on the floor from the previous customers. Several days later, Huso was building a work schedule for Selma and me.

He placed us in different shifts—at first, we would work the same hours, and then she and I alternated days.

The barbershop had a big foot traffic, and it turned out to be the best place to meet people. Our daily visitor was a former soldier named Ibrahim, nicknamed Ibro, who had lost his legs when he came out of the building to inspect where a shell had fallen. A few seconds later, another shell fell nearby, and the shrapnel had severed his legs from his knees down. His legs were amputated and were replaced with prosthetic ones. He walked like a puppet with a cane in his hand, carefully stepping into the barbershop so as not to fall over. Ibro had good and bad days. On good days, he laughed a lot and made jokes with Huso, Selma, and me. Huso took care of him like he was his last customer on earth. He had little hair on his head, but he wore a beard that Huso trimmed carefully and to the perfect length. Then he would put cologne on him. He was a handsome and tall man in his early forties. On his bad days, he was quiet, exhuming a certain attitude that repelled and demanded silence. His brow would be furrowed. He seemed to be so unhappy and angry, and I always assumed it was because such a sudden loss that caused paralysis would drive anyone into rage and despair. His life was limited now. I was careful to choose the right words around him, mainly to make sure I wouldn't piss him off even more.

Ibro was married to a blond, blue-eyed beauty, Senida, who had some kind of function in the army. Sometimes she would come to the barbershop to say hi. She had the energy of five bulls, and she always laughed. She seemed to have taken care of Ibro, but he seemed to be angrier around her. They were like black and white next to each other. Like death and life.

Asim was one of my favorite customers. He drove a green Golf, and he came over for a shave every couple of days. His calm personality was attractive. When he wasn't in a rush, he would ask Selma or me to shave him. One day, I cut his chin, causing him to bleed profusely, and from then on, he refused to be my customer. Eventually, Selma and I built our own clientele. Sometimes, kids our age would come during my shift and ask for Selma, and vice versa. The best benefit about the job was that even if the customers didn't have to pay, they would tip in cigarettes. Most soldiers were generous. Those who didn't smoke would give me an entire pack, and I would be the happiest person on the planet. Cigarettes were also used to bargain for things on the market, if there was anything available.

One day, a young girl came in for a haircut. After I finished cutting her hair, she placed a bunch of cigarettes on the countertop. I formed a big smile when she handed those cigarettes because I hadn't had any for a couple of days. Out of politeness, I responded with a common Bosnian saying: "Oh, you shouldn't have."

She stood up, said okay, took all the cigarettes back, and left. From then on, I had learned my lesson—just to thank the person and not be too nice.

Young soldiers came often, even just for the good company, and Selma and I were always a good reason to visit. Huso was the driver of good humor and positive attitude, but Selma and I were just as silly, goofy, and fun to be around. One time, a soldier asked me for a shave after I gave him a haircut. His face barely had any hair. It was thin and would take only a few strokes to get rid of. When I finished shaving him, I paused and asked, "Does your mom let you put cologne on?"

Everyone in the barbershop burst into laughter. The barbershop eventually became a place to come and relax; it was an oasis in a desert.

But it was not always a good old time in the barbershop. A soldier once came in for a haircut, and as soon as he arrived, he demanded to be served. Huso told him two customers were ahead of him and he had to wait, but he didn't take it lightly.

He got in Huso's face, grabbed his white coat, and began screaming and yelling, "You piece of shit! You better do it now or I'm going to kill you!"

I saw fear in Huso's eyes, as he was shaking and trying to free himself from this man's arms. But the soldier was strong, and the rage in him strengthened him. Huso apologized to the customers who had been waiting and told the soldier to sit down. Silence permeated through the barbershop. When Huso finished cutting his hair, the soldier left, swearing under his breath.

Getting used to bad and grouchy customers didn't come naturally to us. As soon as they stepped foot into the barbershop, the atmosphere would turn tense. The vice commander for the Dobrinja Five brigade would visit often, wearing his black beret, never smiling, and never exchanging niceties with us. One time, I feared he might pull his gun from the side of his uniform and shoot us all. I understood that leading an army of men and organizing battles to protect all of us brought much stress to his life, and this was why we were lenient and more receptive to such negative attitudes. We'd observe, never react, and try to be as empathetic as possible.

When he came to visit one day, he walked around the barbershop, stuck out his pointer finger covered in a leather glove, and touched random surfaces, commenting, "There's dust here." He'd take a couple of steps, choose another random spot, and add, "And here." As he moved around, his finger would get busier, finding dusty spots and point it out to us.

Huso, Selma, and I would freeze and wait for the next moment. *Is he going to shoot us? What is this asshole doing pointing out about dust? Who gives a shit?* It's not like I could say that to him, or I would really get shot.

When he ended his discovery expedition, he turned around and looked Huso in the eye. "By the end of the day, I want to see the entire shop spotless clean, top to bottom. You get that?"

"Yes, sir. Selma, Nadija, why don't you focus on cleaning the shop right away?" Huso tried to show his leadership.

Vice Commander's colleague, Muhamed, the army commander, seemed somewhat friendlier and never demanded such things from us. He also preferred his hair done after hours, when the shop was about to close. When things in the neighborhood were going well and no recent deaths had been reported, Muhamed was in a good mood, chatting and laughing with us. But when too many soldiers were lost on the battlefield, we learned to keep our distance. One day, when he came to visit, I was sitting outside with a spray bottle filled with water, and when I saw him, I sprayed him in a playful gesture. He went inside the barbershop and started screaming and yelling at Huso for having workers who misbehaved. He chastised me, as if I pulled a gun on him. I learned my lesson that there were probably more bad than good days on his duty as a commander. Muhamed was one of the most strategic and toughest Dobrinja army commanders.

We eventually learned he also had a soft side. One day, he came in to get his hair done. Huso usually had Selma or me help with a customer, but for the big shots or people he highly respected, we weren't allowed near them. To my surprise, before Huso began, he offered me stay and help. I stayed since that option seemed more exciting. Muhamed had Huso lock the door so no one could interrupt. To my further surprise, Huso pulled out curlers and perm solution and started working on Muhamed's hair. Huso usually asked his customers what type of haircut or style they wanted, but not this time. It seemed as if he had done this many times before. Once Huso curled Muhamed's hair, he put a pink cover on Muhamed's head. I wanted to burst out laughing when I saw how silly it looked against his green uniform, but I contained myself. They made me swear I wouldn't tell anyone that he had just gotten a perm. I felt like a soldier who had to keep the military top secret.

The best thing about working in a barbershop was that Selma and

I had access to many supplies to play with our hair. We had perms regularly; we colored our bangs blond; we colored our hair red and then back to brown again, and, most excitingly, we could wash our hair with running water.

An army battalion Delta was stationed in Vogošće, a part of Sarajevo that was a twenty-minute car ride from Dobrinja. The Delta soldiers often came to Dobrinja to fight in the battles for the neighborhood. They were young, and all looked the same, as if they had come out from a production line. Sometimes I couldn't tell who was who even though they had introduced themselves. A soldier once told me I looked like the famous singer Tanita Tikaram, and I was offended because I didn't think she was good-looking. Huso told us one day that the Delta commander invited us to come to the army headquarters where we would cut soldiers' hair. We closed the shop for a day and got a ride to Vogošće. I was excited about the opportunity, as it was my first time leaving Dobrinja since my stay in Vratnik. Leaving Dobrinja felt like an award-winning event on so many levels. You got to feel the air outside of your confined space; you got to be reminded that Sarajevo stood still proudly, and, finally, that you survived the trip intact. When we arrived at the army headquarters, several soldiers greeted us outside and, like vultures, circled around us, saying hello. They set up three chairs—one for Huso, Selma, and me—so that the soldiers could take turns getting a haircut. I was all business, taking my job seriously. I finally felt like I had a purpose during the war. When I arrived home, my mother gave me a hard time because I had not informed her I would leave Dobrinja for a day. It all happened so fast. We were summoned practically on a whim, and I didn't have time to run back to the house and tell her the plan for the day.

At one point, a young hairstylists' competition was organized in Dobrinja Three. Every competitor was to find a male model and cut his hair, and the judges would determine the winner. I asked our neighbor from across the street to be my model. He had thick and healthy hair—the type that wasn't too stubborn and was fairly easy to manage. There were six or seven of us in the competition. The judges were Huso, his old friend, also an accomplished hairstylist, and another barber. We had an hour to complete the task—to cut the hair, to dry it, to style it, and finally to showcase it. When I finished, my model's hair looked nearly perfect. An hour later, they announced the winners. In the first place came Selma, and I came in third. When they announced the winners, they had us walk out on the stage to accept our prize. I won twenty-five convertible marks, a new Bosnian currency, and a chocolate bar. Even though I had promised my model I would share my prize with him, I didn't. I was angry and disappointed that I came in third even though my model's haircut looked better than Selma's. Back in the barbershop, we were all sitting down, having a smoke, reflecting on the competition, and Huso's friend pointed his finger at me and said, "I think you... you should have won."

Huso waved his hand and replied, "What can you do now? No big deal." I couldn't help but think it was all a setup, considering Huso was close friends with Selma's parents.

Once everyone in the neighborhood heard that Selma was number one, they all wanted her to cut their hair. Or, did my model tell everyone what a cheapskate, a promise breaker I was, making everyone disgusted with me? I would understand if my model told everyone, as I later regretted not keeping my promise to share the prize with him. But I felt good about earning money. I spent it on new sneakers.

None of this mattered, as I was making customers on the side. All my close friends and my family members had me cut their hair. When friends of friends heard about my skills, I became quite popular and in high demand.

The barbershop was turning into a serious business as the war progressed. A hairstyling school in Dobrinja was sending students to the shop to serve as interns, and at one point, there were nine of us. Huso became stricter about the rules, and he had our schedules planned out and written in a notebook. Our work schedules turned from full days to a block of hours on certain days, so everyone worked. Meanwhile, Huso's wife was growing suspicious of Huso and she'd constantly call the shop to check up on his whereabouts. When Selma answered the phone, she'd caught his wife in the middle of a sentence, yelling from the top of her lungs.

Selma would put the receiver against her arm and look at me. "It's her again."

"Oh. What is she saying?"

"She's calling us sluts. What should I do?" Selma was unsure.

"Hang up!"

CHAPTER 14

Reunion with Jasmina

*I*n war, you win or lose, live or die—and the difference is just an eyelash.
—Douglas MacArthur

DURING 1993, phones lines functioned again and Jasmina and I had reestablished our connection. We talked on the phone often in order to catch up with the happenings in our lives. At that point, she had made a whole new set of friends while I had as well. She now lived in a part of the city, Alipašino Polje, which was a couple of kilometers past the Mojmilo hill, a close distance from Dobrinja. She, her parents, and her brother had moved to an apartment on the ninth floor. The apartment had a view of the main street in Sarajevo that stretched to downtown and the stone-made TV station where her father worked as a chef. I wanted to know all about her life and how she had been surviving this crazy war since I last saw her. We would share our stories, tips, and tricks on food recipes, ways to master school subjects, and all things teenage.

I invited her to come over one day, with the caution that Dobrinja was the most unstable part of the city and unpredictable as far as shelling. The people of Dobrinja had learned the shelling patterns by then. We all knew that the shooting on weekends was more intense because, for the men from Serbia and Montenegro, war was a part-time job. We called them weekenders. I told her she should rather pick a weekday when it was quieter and there was a lesser risk of being shot.

Once she finally mustered up the courage, she appeared in front of our door one day. It was one of the happiest days of the war. I had not seen Jasmina since downtown at Hotel Europe more than a year ago. Reconnecting with my lifelong friend felt like going back home where I could sleep in my bed under clean linens, where I could watch the planes ascend into the sky, or where I could call Jasmina on a whim to go outside and make up our games. These reminders helped revive the memories of the blissful childhood when the days were carefree. Sadness came over me because I felt and knew a lot had changed. Jasmina was not the same person as before. She had become more serious, quiet in her speech, pensive, and careful about her next words. We sat in my room, and something strange happened. While on the phone, we would talk nonstop, cutting each other off and gasping for the next word or topic. Face-to-face, we ran out of words. We just stared at each other, occasionally ducking our heads, hiding our eyes from sadness and disbelief that the war had changed us so much. It was almost as if I had just met another person. I didn't know who she really was. Could I trust her? Would she reveal all my secrets I had whispered to her over the phone? And what about her looks? She had aged, looked taller, one of her teeth was broken. This was not the same Jasmina I once knew.

We giggled as we awkwardly sat across from each other, waiting for the other to break the silence.

In her usual humorous style, she finally uttered, "We should have brought our phone receivers and pretend like we're talking on the phone."

We laughed, and a sense of relief came over us. This was the

Jasmina I knew. When she broke the silence, which seemed to last forever, she was telling me about her friends, high school dilemmas, the times she almost got killed by a shell, and all other war-related topics too common in homes.

Jasmina and I saw each other more often. She came one day so I could give her a haircut. She had fine curly hair, but I accepted the challenge of making her haircut look good. As long as I had known Jasmina, her nickname was Seka, which meant "little sister" in Bosnian. Perhaps because she grew up tiny and fragile? When her hair grew long, it looked too big for her small head. When she showed up at the barbershop that day, I proudly cut her hair to show what I had accomplished in the past year. But her hair seemed so difficult to manage. I cut it on the right side, then on the left side, and then, since the hair seemed uneven, I cut it on the right side again, and then again on the left.

When Huso saw me struggling, he paused from cutting his customer's hair, walked up to me, and said, "Look what you did. You made a little brother out of little sister."

We all had a big laugh about it. But I felt bad for not living up to my expectation. Jasmina found Huso funny and didn't seem to share any concerns about her haircut. She was a good sport.

"It will grow back," she said to make me feel better. Eventually, I was meeting her friends; her, mine, and our worlds collided again. She still smoked heavily, something we shared in common. I also had discovered that like me, she liked to have a drink or two even though alcohol was scarce and only to be found at parties.

Jasmina and I shared a lot of experiences growing up together since we lived door to door. Her mother often told us a story when she took the pacifiers out of our mouths—Jasmina was two years old and I one—and threw them in the trash. That was how far back our friendship lived. When we were growing up, our parents couldn't always afford to buy us new clothes, so every time they bought something new for us, it was a treat. As Amra was growing out of her clothes, I would often end up inheriting them as hand-me-downs, whether I liked it. But my parents were practical and wanted to ensure that all new clothes saw the full circle of life, which meant Amra's clothes were destined to land on me. When it was our time for new clothes treat, Jasmina and I made our moms coordinate in buying the same shoes, same overalls, same plaid shirts, but in different colors. We often looked like sisters, even though we didn't have similar facial features.

When we became teenagers, we got into the shady business of going downtown to a club called KUK, designed for people older than us, mostly medical students whose college was above the club. Our curfew was ten o'clock, so we ventured out to KUK around eight, showed up around eight thirty just as it opened up, hung out for about an hour, and then headed back home when the crowd thickened. We thought of ourselves as cool, listening to punk rock and alternative music, although Jasmina was much more educated in music than me. On our way to the club, we made up songs, mainly about our adventures in meeting different people and our trips to KUK.

> Sijalica, sijalica, sijalica
> Sijalica, sijalica, sijalica,
> Sijalica, to je KUK!
>
> Lightbulb, lightbulb, lightbulb
> Lightbulb, lightbulb, lightbulb
> Lightbulb, that is KUK!

These lyrics were inspired after meeting the friendly manager of KUK, whose head we thought was shaped like a lightbulb.

One night, we showed up in our blue winter ski jackets, which we took off as soon as we stepped in, as we feared we wouldn't look cool enough wearing them. We sat next to a guy who was the grandson and namesake of a famous writer and author, Mak Dizdar. Both Jasmina and I found him attractive, with his tall, lean body, blond hair, blue eyes, and beard sparingly showing on his nicely featured face. He looked like Kurt Cobain to me. He was into metal music—might have been a drug addict, it was hard to tell—but we found him super cool and wanted to be close in his proximity whenever we had a chance. That night, he sat in a corner of a bench all alone and drank beer from a bottle. In order to create an opportunity to talk to him, one of us suggested asking if he will share a sip with us. But who is going to ask? You ask. No, you ask. What am I gonna say? Just say, Hey, can we try your beer? And so Jasmina did. Without hesitation, he extended his arm with the beer in his hand and let us try it. The taste was extremely bitter, even for a watered-down lager.

Yugoslavia didn't impose a drinking age, so it didn't matter that I was only thirteen and Jasmina fourteen.

Whether that was the culprit of my alcohol drinking, I do not know, but that was the first time I tried alcohol. During the war, alcohol was a refuge from the dire circumstances. I drank alcohol during the war every chance I got, hoping to relieve the anxiety. It was my medication, helping me forget I was living in a pressure cooker, nowhere to go, nothing to live for but survival, and no clear future.

The people Jasmina and I hung out with almost all drank alcohol. We'd look for house parties where most of the drinking took place. And there were many. Before the party, we'd wander around with our friends and find places to smoke. Our friend nicknamed Cinda, a hard-core punk rock fan with a prominent dark gel-covered mohawk on his small stature, and also a leader of the Sarajevo soccer club fan base *Horde Zla*, would find weed somewhere and go places he'd hide from other weed smokers in scarcity. We'd find a park, sit on busted benches, and talk. I had just met Cinda, and I learned that, despite his perceived wildness and maybe aggression as a club fan leader and mohawk carrier, he was friendly, always wearing a smile.

To make our conversation interesting, Jasmina turned to me and asked, "What do you think is Cinda's real name? Think of a flower."

"Hmmm. Iris?" They laughed.

"Do I look like a girl?" Cinda had a good sense of humor and didn't take any offense at my guess.

"Or, sorry. So what is it?"

"It's Narcis." It meant 'a daffodil' in Bosnian.

Cinda would get high, and we'd then venture out to a party. Word spread quickly among friends when there was a party, and Jasmina and I would show up whether we knew everyone or no one. Since the curfew began at ten at night and lasted until five in the morning, these parties lasted all night. On a rare occasion the host had a power generator, we could listen to music from a stereo. Often, it was metal music such as Metallica. Pearl Jam's "Alive" was a favorite.

We would all sing in unison, some half drunk, some completely wasted. We listened to metal music, as if to signal the madness—to live vicariously through its sheer words of anger, pain, and suffering. There was Iron Maiden and Sepultura, and we channeled our anger and despair through their songs, and it helped. We banged our heads as we sat on the floor, and in between bangs, we passed the beer around for everyone to share. With the loud music, we couldn't hear the shooting. It sheltered us from the cruel world outside.

I did not know where the alcohol came from during the war. At some point, Sarajevska Pivara, the local brewery, might have produced limited amounts of beer, making it more difficult to get ahold of, but it happened. And often, we would run out of alcohol in the middle of the party and think of ways to get more, but with no luck. At one party, alcohol was plentiful, but we ran out of water, which spoiled the evening, as we couldn't use the bathroom or wash our hands. How ironic.

In the morning, after partying all night long, Jasmina and I would drag ourselves to her place, where a sleepover was more than welcome. Public transportation didn't function, so we walked every-where, all the time. Sometimes, we'd sleep over at a party host's place, finding a lonesome corner where we'd curl up and wait for the sun to rise. Over the years during the war, we learned to sleep on various surfaces. Soft bed, hard bed, no mattress, short mattress, no bed, firm pillow, no pillow. Sometimes, we'd end up sleeping next to a person we hardly knew, sometimes hugging each other for some unknown comfort of being human and realizing we were all trapped in this dangerous maze together.

Over time, I forgot what a comfortable bed looked and felt like. At my age, I could easily handle discomforts and restless sleep, although my asthma was getting worse and would often wake me up in the middle of the night, making me gasp for air.

I stayed over at Jasmina's one night, and my asthma acted up. She woke up, listening to my wheezing. In a panic, she asked me if there was anything she could do for me. No. She could not. My only escape route was to stand up and ensure I was breathing air in and that my lungs had enough strength to expand as I waited for the storm to pass.

As time went on and more parties took place, Jasmina and I strengthened our bond again. While it was not the same as before, in some ways, it was better. We were teenagers now, longing to belong somewhere, to live life to the fullest, learn together, and experience the world with open arms. At one point, all our friends, as well as those who knew of us, expected us to arrive together wherever we showed up. If either of us was alone, the question often seemed to be, "And where is your other half?"

And yet, as much as we shared the same view of the world, we were different. Jasmina was known for her goofy sense of humor. I was known as one to always be quiet, almost never uttering a word until I was drunk by the time social interaction ensued. Together, we were welcomed in all social circles during the siege of Sarajevo. This reunion made me realize it was one of the best things that happened to us during the war.

CHAPTER 15

To Enlist or Not to Enlist

*W*e shall defend our island, whatever the cost may be, we shall fight on the beaches, we shall fight on the landing grounds, we shall fight in the fields and in the streets, we shall fight in the hills; we shall never surrender.

—Winston Churchill

IN 1994, the public transportation—electric trollies and trams—resumed working when the intermittent power was on. Everything about war seemed to have been normalized. War was no longer the major topic of discussion like it was in the beginning. Dying of bullets and shells became normal. It was such a frequent occurrence that I thought no one would ever die of a natural death again. We couldn't fathom someone dying from a heart attack or diabetes or another fatal illness.

In the spring, someone gave my mother seeds for different vegetables, and she quickly claimed a piece of land behind the building to plant and grow them. Soon we had spinach, onions, tomatoes, and potatoes growing like weeds. The vegetables made an immediate difference in our diet. The onion alone made our food taste much better. We could now make a potato pie without substituting potatoes with rice. The fresh vegetables made me feel as if a small slice of peace had arrived.

Even though Sarajevo was still under siege, shells weren't falling as often, and getting to downtown Sarajevo became much easier. The Bosnian Army had taken back some of the land along the main street in Dobrinja and put up large concrete blocks along the street to add more protection for pedestrians. At the beginning of May, my mother received a phone call from her boss, summoning her to work immediately. She worked in human resources at the TV station, which fortunately was close to Dobrinja. Now that the tram worked again, my mother would go visit Vratnik after work and sleep over at her mother's place. Amra, Anis, and I had the place to ourselves when my father was on sentry duty. I dreaded these times, as I felt like a third wheel.

During the day, I'd escape and go visit our neighbor, Ifeta, on the second floor. Ifeta was a young widow, previously married to Esad, who died as a soldier in a battle in the Serbian village. They had two young children, Dada and Minela, and the older was born when Ifeta was only seventeen. The whole family was tall, and her husband had towered over us. Esad was always cheerful. He was originally from the eastern part of Bosnia, Goražde. My mother and Esad often teased each other, and they laughed all the time. The day he died, the house had become eerily quiet, and his children were unsettled. Minela had eventually turned into a mini monster, while Dada was quiet and Ifeta was crying all the time. My mother went to visit her often to keep her company and consoler her, but there was only so much a person could do to make a young widow less sad.

Ifeta was a heavy smoker, and she chain-smoked to calm her nerves. Amra and I sought reasons to visit her in order to smoke, hidden from our mother. Our plan was to alternate the times we smoked, because if my mother suddenly paid a visit, we wouldn't be surprised with a cigarette in our hands. When she entered Ifeta's apartment, we would put down the cigarette in the ashtray, and Ifeta would grab it, claiming it as hers. My mother, who was a devout nonsmoker before the war, was now a smoker ever since Coco came to visit us in the beginning of the war, and she helped herself to a cigarette from his pack. The war made us develop unhealthy, quirky habits. But my mother didn't smoke properly. She either never learned how to do it or refused to inhale all the way into her lungs. When she exhaled the smoke, an enormous cloud would form in front of her, and you could barely see her face.

One time when she visited Ifeta's, Amra and I were annoyed, as we had just lit a cigarette. One of us asked harshly, "Why are you here?"

She said nothing, and she cried, storming out of Ifeta's place. I felt bad. This was not how our parents taught us to behave. Our words were uncalled for.

Around that same time, Sabaheta and her sons returned to their home in Dobrinja because Sabaheta didn't get along well with her mother.

Out of the blue, Emir, Sabaheta's son, got a hold of a pistol. His neighbor from the first floor sold it to him. After Uncle Ramiz passed away, Emir hated everything about Serbs. He wanted to take revenge for his father's death, and all he did was daydream about killing Serbs. He was still a teenager, with a lot more growing up to do, and too young to join the army. Even if he was old enough, Sabaheta would use her connections to get him excused from duty. She couldn't handle it. She couldn't handle another loss. When I came over to visit, he'd pull out his pistol and show it off like it was a lollipop he was about to lick. He'd point at certain parts of the living room and pretend he was about to shoot.

I'd tell him, "Get that out of my sight. You're crazy."

On top of everything, he became a fanatic about Islam and began to pray and go to the mosque every day. He looked down on us for not following the religion the way he did, and we all thought he should mind his own business.

Sabaheta tried to take control of the situation, but he wouldn't listen. She hated being a single parent now. She had to take care of them as both the mother and the father, but it didn't always work.

Emir didn't have the same respect for her as he did for his father. To get to his senses, she'd often yell at him.

"Are you going crazy? What is wrong with you? We've never been religious. Why are you pretending to be a big Muslim now? That's not how we raised you!"

"Serbs killed my father. They need to pay for it."

"And what are you going to do? What are you going to do with that single pistol? Give me a break!"

During the day, he'd walk around the neighborhood with some of his other fanatic friends, wearing an Arabic kaffiyah scarf that someone gave him. Of all his friends, he was the worst. I got a sense he wanted to be the leader of the pack and that everyone would follow him. Some of us agreed he was losing his mind. When Emir turned eighteen, he was required to enlist in the army. But Sabaheta got him out of it by providing medical records to show he was incapable. I was surprised. What? Emir had only one kidney?

There were two kinds of people in the war. One that firmly believed in defending our country and fighting hard for the Bosnian people. The other kind was fearful of losing their life, which was highly probable. Some people, like my father, were not fully capable or fit to serve. My father had always had high blood pressure, trouble with kidney stones, and poor night vision, among other health complications. So men would either do anything to enlist in the army and act upon their patriotism or do anything to get out of it. My father wrote letters, drafts written in the back of our recipe notebook, addressing his inabilities to perform as a soldier and trying to collect all his medical records to prove it. While the records stood a chance, the bureaucracy made the process slower and harder. It didn't matter that 1994 was easier to endure than the previous years. For my father, sitting in a trench during wintry nights did not seem like the best use of his time, especially since he claimed to be a hazard himself.

My father despised being a soldier. This war was not his to fight. He was not willing to sacrifice his home, his youth, or his children's prospects for someone else's ideals. He never felt the war was instigated by Muslims or that the Serbs' attack was warranted. It was taking a toll on him and he grew angrier and angrier as his hope plunged overtime. My parents' yelling, the way they usually communicated before the war, became increasingly more intense and unbearable. My father would come home from sentry duty and complain about insignificant things, like one day a neighbor my age walked by him and spit close to my father's proximity. He'd be annoyed by it and complain to us how rude and inconsiderate the young man was. Where were his manners? My mother would react by shouting back, and they would quickly get into a fight. My mother was a soldier in her own way—protecting her children as best as possible by providing them with food and shelter during the tough times.

Together, I saw them as two soldiers who had already lost many individual battles, but were hoping to win a war as one, constantly hanging on by a thread.

Around June 1994, he was finally released from the army and immediately called to report into work. My father worked for the government in the veteran affairs department, sorting out benefits for surviving soldiers from World War II. A couple of years before the war, he was told that his department might shut down soon as veterans were slowly dying out, and the need to serve them ceased. But now, his job seemed safer than ever, as he would be busy with managing benefits for a new line of surviving soldiers and their families. His work building downtown was shelled down to the foundation the first year of the war, so his office was temporarily moved to a different location, an abandoned furniture store. As transportation was spotty, depending on electricity and shooting, he would have to walk several kilometers and back. He often stayed downtown and slept over at his mother's place in order to make his commute easier the following day. The days were scattered with our parents taking turns sleeping over at their parents' place. Their absence reminded me of the times Amra and I yearned to be home alone, but that was no longer the case. During the war, I felt a void.

CHAPTER 16

Moon

I am tired and sick of war. Its glory is all moon-shine. It is only those who have neither fired a shot nor heard the shrieks and groans of the wounded who cry aloud for blood, for vengeance, for desolation. War is hell.
—William Tecumseh Sherman

ONE DAY, Anis surprised us by bringing a dog home. His apartment was empty most of the time, so he kept the dog there. His cousin Emina, who always wanted to become a vet, had the dog, and she had to get rid of him. She named him Moon, but there was nothing Moony about him. He was a big black schnauzer, with a laid-back attitude, who refused to follow commands. Anis found a book about schnauzers and encouraged us to read it so we could learn more about our new pet. He was a temperamental and stubborn kind, and it showed through and through.

"Moon, sit. Moon, stand up. Moon, lie down."

He'd usually just stare at us as if he thought we were going insane.

He immediately became popular among our neighbors, and everyone wanted to play with him when he was friendly. He sometimes barked at people and occasionally chased them, so he was slowly losing the reputation of being a nice, good-natured dog. Since food was scarce, we grabbed whatever leftover the army kitchen had at the end of the day. The dog ate rice and beans most of the time.

We kept him in Anis's apartment unless we took him out for a walk. When we hung out in the apartment, Moon would place his front paws on the windowsill facing the garage and bark madly. A few minutes later, shells would fall nearby. We thought Moon could predict forthcoming danger, so when we heard him bark, we made ourselves ready for an enemy attack. Moon was hyperactive, and the minute you came into the apartment, he'd jump on you, run back and forth, jump on you again, and his enormous body would make you lose balance and tip you over. Sometimes, we'd find his poop sitting in the hallway, typically on the days we couldn't attend to him earlier because either we were too busy to take him out or shelling was taking place.

But Moon wasn't always hyperactive. One day, I went to Anis's apartment because I needed some time alone. At that point, I was losing hope the war would ever end. In that realization, fear came over me as I questioned whether there was a resolution to this craziness. Sarajevo was still exposed to danger, and we had no way out of this madness. In the summer, the stench of corpses wafted through the air. The soldiers who got killed on the Mojmilo hill were still lying dead after years had passed because no one could go up there and remove the remains. The Serbs maintained an open view of the hill from the village and could shoot anytime.

I went downstairs and found Moon lying quietly in the living room. I sat next to him and cried. He lifted his head and looked at me as I cried, and he gently put his head down again and closed his eyes.

I caressed him and whispered, "I'm so depressed, Moon. I know you don't understand what I'm saying now. Whatever. I tell you, I'm too tired of this stupid war."

I had convinced myself it was depression I was feeling, but it was more of an angst. There was no time to feel depressed in survival mode.

I would sit down with Moon for hours. He would place his paws on my legs and lie still the whole time.

Moon was a strange character. Sometimes I felt connected to him, and I felt he really understood me. When I went to the window to see what was going on outside, he would insist on standing next to me with his paws up on the windowsill while I chatted with our neighbors. Chatting wasn't my biggest forte, but I exchanged a few words here and there. Oliver, a neighbor from across the street, the dentist's son, came over to talk to me one day, and he asked me about Moon. I talked, and Oliver said something like "You have a pleasant smile, but too bad you have crooked teeth. You'd be much prettier if you fixed your teeth, you know." Moon started barking at him, and Oliver slowly walked away. Moon was my protector, in a way.

But sometimes I didn't feel so connected to the dog. When I took him out for a walk, he would pull me with all his strength, and I had to run behind him to keep up. He cared little that I lacked the strength in my arms. Over time, he found a scheme to escape. Sometimes, when Anis took him out, he would let him run without a leash. As soon as he was let go, Moon would start to run and keep running and running and running until we could no longer catch him. He'd be caught in city trams, terrifying people with his size and stature, as people feared he might bite.

It was as if he was angry at us for leaving him alone in Anis's apartment for long periods of time. He wanted to punish us and never see our sorry asses again. And repeatedly, Anis or someone else would catch him. Luckily, Moon was returned home every time he tried to escape. Unlucky for him.

A neighbor caught Anis with Moon one time, standing in the garage and attempting to train him. Anis had broken his pointer finger, and it was wrapped in a cast.

His finger was pointing toward the ceiling while he was screaming from the top of his lungs at Moon, "Moon, sit. Moon, sit. Moon, you stupid dog, sit!"

Moon would just stare at him, bark occasionally, and not cave in.

When Anis and Amra toyed with the idea of getting married, they decided to live in Anis's apartment once they got hitched. The tradeoff for the marriage was getting rid of Moon. There was no way they could live with the dog and keep the apartment clean. Over time, the smell from Moon was so bad that my father didn't want to set foot in the apartment. He'd call the place *Munovina*, Moon-shit. Anis asked around if anyone wanted Moon, but there were no takers. Desperate to get rid of him, he finally came up with the only workable solution —to let him go. Before he headed to sentry duty, he told me, "Nadija, take him today and just let him go. He will just run, and you won't have to worry."

* * *

The day was beautiful and sunny. August 1994, summer. Moon and I walked a few hundred feet from the building. Before I released the leash, I gave him a quick hug. I set him free and expected him to gallop down the street, but a strange thing happened. He wouldn't move. I'd nudge him and say, "Okay, Moon, you're free to go now."

But he just stood there. I walked a little more with him, and then I turned around and walked in the opposite direction. But when I turned around to see where he was, he was still standing there.

"Go, Moon, go! You're free to go!" I encouraged him again. He slowly walked until his steps sped up. He'd stop, look at me again, turn around, and keep walking. I disappeared around the building and could no longer see his attempt to leave.

Amra and Anis cleaned the apartment from top to bottom and opened all the windows to replace the Moon-shit with fresh air. They kept the windows open all night.

Shortly after, we heard that someone captured Moon and took him in. The new owner had a hamburger store and was some kind of tough guy you didn't want to mess with. He named him something different; he was no longer Moon. Being his old self, Moon kept escaping from his new owner and indulging himself, running along the tram tracks or, on a good day, on a tram itself, harassing people and scaring them off. The new owner didn't want to put up with Moon's bullshit, so when he finally got him back, he shot him with his pistol. He died instantly. When I found out, I cried. Moon didn't deserve to die.

CHAPTER 17

❦

Boys

War is fear cloaked in courage.
—William Westmoreland

AS MY PUBERTY MATERIALIZED, my interest in boys became more serious. When I worked at the barbershop, I had access to one of the best barbers in Sarajevo, Huso. Selma and I would think of new hairdos and ask Huso to do it for us. How about a perm? What about red hair? How about a highlight in the bangs? We would look like the folk singer Halid Muslimović, who everybody made fun of for his blond highlight in the front, but it might look good. Although the war was raging, women wanted to look good. As the war kept on, we had more and more women as our customers.

I was showing signs of becoming a woman. My breasts grew, and they were becoming more visible in the absence of a bra. One time, when a few boys noticed I wasn't wearing one (there really wasn't a place to get one), they told me to run toward them. When I ran, I noticed they were staring at my bosom and laughed, so I stopped running immediately and pulled on my shirt to hide the little slopes underneath. I was embarrassed and might have told them off. I cared more about my looks, as I realized I wanted to look good for myself and the neighborhood boys. I didn't have many love interests—it wasn't really my thing—but I enjoyed the company of my male companions.

At some point, I hung out with a group of boys my age—Goran, Igor, Bojan, and Nadir—who got together at an abandoned apartment close to the enemy line. In order to get from one part of the building to another without going outside, the people who lived in the building knocked down the walls between units on the ground floor. We would climb through several holes until we arrived at the apartment that was the last stop in the building. The enemy side of the building was abandoned. It was destroyed, walls barely hanging on, and apartments void of the furniture and life. The apartment where we hung out was safe, as it was protected by sandbags and was facing the Muslim village across the Dobrinja stream. I was the only girl to hang out in the apartment. Nadir, Bojan, Igor, and Goran became my buddies. We would sit on uninviting chairs and couch that were soaked by rain. We didn't care. Bojan was a tall boy who had a dream of becoming a professional drummer. He would often bang his legs and knees with his palms to create sounds and rhythms. In our conversations, we mostly talked about music. Nadir had long greasy hair, split down the middle, and he loved talking about musicians such as Ozzy Osborne, his favorite. Igor was a metal head. He loved Slayer and Metallica, and he often sang songs although his voice was terrible and his English accent even worse. Goran was a boy who laughed all the time. His mother was my Bosnian teacher, somewhat tough, but I could tell she wanted to raise Goran to be a kind man, which he was.

Being a tomboy as a child, I didn't mind hanging out with the boys. I fit in. But one day, it hit me that hanging out with the boys made absolutely no sense to me. What could I gain from talking about music? I knew little about music. I listened to former Yugoslav rock and roll music, when all the kids my age preferred to listen to New Kids on the Block and Vanilla Ice. I was the girl everyone thought of as cool because I looked confident, but I barely ever spoke in groups unless I knew the group well and was comfortable. I was turning into a cute girl, but I always had the fear of people laughing at my crooked teeth, so I barely smiled or laughed and kept conversations to a minimum.

When I realized that hanging out with the boys seemed pointless and a waste of time, I decided I would skip the visit. Around six o'clock, the phone rang, and it was Nadir, asking my mother where I was and why I hadn't shown up. I signaled my mom to tell him I wasn't feeling well, but I loved they cared for me, for my presence. The following day, I showed up, and everything went back to the same old routine.

Shortly after, I found out that Igor had a crush on me. He was cute, a bit too skinny, around my height, and Amra's age. His father was a local soldier who always wore his uniform, whether it was a day of duty, with a knife on one side of his pants and a pistol on the other. You knew immediately his father was present because he talked loudly with the neighbors and made fun of anyone who crossed his path. Despite having little interest in dating Igor, I spent more time with him. He came from a nice family. His mother was our biology professor, and his younger brother, who didn't look like either of his parents, had a puberty mutating voice that made us laugh when he spoke in class. Igor had a deep voice and was a spitting image of his father. He was too young to be a soldier, but he was always wearing uniform pants, a T-shirt, and a plaid shirt on top.

As we spent more time together, I sensed Igor had a crush on me. He would look at me with his bright blue eyes, caress my hair, and say nice and sweet things. But in every attempt to kiss me, I would dodge his advance and pretend that I wasn't ready for the next move. He would often get frustrated and raise his voice, trying to tell me that this was the right thing to do and that he really wanted to kiss me. But I wouldn't budge. My fear of kissing from the time the young boy made fun of me was lingering and constantly whispering in my ear that, if I kissed again, I would be subject to humiliation. I wasn't falling for him, even though I found him cool and possibly even attractive.

I was sixteen. When I was growing up, my mother kept preaching to Amra and me that losing virginity at a young age and having meaningless unprotected sex was out of the question. My mother's words carried a lot of weight when I was young. She was the dominant figure in our upbringing. If my father raised his voice at us, Amra and I found it unacceptable, out of character. She told us drugs were evil. Never use drugs, or you could kiss your life goodbye. But as the war progressed, there wasn't much of advice or words of wisdom coming from either of my parents. I realized that living in extreme circumstances, the only advice given was to be careful walking outside, even though that was a moot point. Everyone knew that shelling came at unpredictable times, and you could escape it or walk right into it, and it didn't matter if you ran or walked. Here, my parents couldn't advise me how to handle my situation with Igor. I liked him, but I didn't like him strongly enough to risk my dignity and kiss him.

It all ended one day when he was forceful in trying to kiss me, and in my defense, I instinctively raised my leg and landed it against his sack. He moaned and bent over in obvious pain. I ran away, leaving him there alone, feeling a little regret for what had just occurred. The following day, when I saw his father in his usual fizzy mood, he gave me a hard time for hitting his son.

"I heard what you did to my son. You want him to become fatherless?"

I said nothing in return, but I knew my relationship with Igor was over. And so were the hangouts with the boys. Occasionally, I would take walks with Bojan, and we would chat about many things while he was drumming against his legs or chest.

My genuine interest in a boy didn't come until I met Damir, who lived next door to Keko and Munevera. Dado was tall, had wide shoulders and beautiful blue eyes, and exuded manhood. Later, I learned that a couple of girls in my high school had a crush on him, as he was not only good-looking but also considered funny and friendly. His mother, a single parent, was a pharmacist, and her body was always covered in greasy creams. She worked for a company that made beauty products, and therefore her natural tendencies to use these creams came to light. When Amra and I lived with Keko and Munevera, Dado lived with his aunt downtown. When the connection from Dobrinja to the city was made in 1993, Dado returned home, albeit making frequent trips to the city to stay overnight. He had several high school friends downtown, and they often threw house parties.

I first met Dado on a quiet day when I went to visit Keko and Munevera. Dado was home, and he came to visit Keko. He was sitting on the couch with a lit cigarette in his hand, and he immediately stood up to introduce himself. I noticed how tall and handsome he was. We sat down and chatted for a while, and when it was time for me to leave, Dado offered to walk a circle around the buildings to get to know me better. I had agreed. As luck would have it, the afternoon was peaceful, only a few bullets heard from afar. When it was time to say goodbye, Dado gave me a couple of phones numbers, and I gave him mine so that we could keep in touch. By then, phones worked all the time, and Dobrinja had established a connection with the rest of the city.

As time went on, Dado would come home more frequently and hang out at Anis's place on the ground floor with us. I was too uncomfortable calling Dado, so Amra did it for me. Amra and I had similar voices. When we were kids, the family members and parents' friends often confused us. My mother's best friend, Behka, had called one day before the war, and I answered the phone. "Is this Amrica?" She used the diminutive for her name. She adored Amra.

"No, it's Nadijica," I'd answer.

If Dado answered the phone, she'd chat with him for a bit and then hand me the phone. If his mother answered the phone, she'd pretend it was me and then ask to speak with Dado. He visited often, but every time we were left alone, the same problem would persist. He would reach out to kiss me, but I would turn my head away and pretend like I didn't realize his intent.

On one occasion, when the power was on, we listened to "Seek and Destroy," a song by Metallica, and Dado grabbed me to say, "I found you, and now I will destroy you," as if inserting humor would make things easier. But when he tried to kiss me again, I turned my head away.

I felt awful. I felt the urge to tell him I had a fear of kissing, but I was afraid of losing him. Maybe he would think I was a loser with no experience with boys or that he might laugh at me and proclaim me as a waste of his time? But the more times I turned away, the more he was getting frustrated, in a somewhat cool and measured way.

One day, he said, "You're just so hopeless."

I said nothing in return. No argument. Not a word back. His visits became less frequent until he finally showed up and broke up with me. When he came over to deliver the news, I reacted as if he just told me, "Hey, the sky is blue." He was perplexed about my reaction, or a lack thereof, why there were no feelings attached to the perceived loss.

Shortly after, I heard from him to say that he wanted me back. Apparently, he missed me, and he wanted to give it a second chance. By then, he had introduced me to his high school friends, and although I said little in their presence, I felt assimilated with the group. Often, this was the case during the war. We all felt like one, and no judgments were cast upon others; only love and acceptance.

One day, when Dado was away downtown, he pulled a prank on me. While he was in the company of his friends, he would call me and put me on the phone speaker so that all of his friends could listen in our conversation. I was sleeping when the phone rang. Somberly, still waking up, I picked up the phone. On the other line was Dado.

"Hi, it's Dado." I could hear whispers and giggles in the background.

I paused for a second and, in all sincerity, answered, "Dado who?"

Laughter broke out, and Dado's response was immediate: "Let me call you back."

Despite trying to get closer, Dado and I never kissed. He broke up with me again and let me go, this time forever.

* * *

Out of the blue one day, Enis came into our lives. He was an older guy who lived a few blocks away in our old neighborhood. My mom and his mom were colleagues at the TV station. His brother and father were both killed the day Serbs occupied the neighborhood. Enis witnessed their murders. One evening, he showed up in our apartment with his friend from college. It was Anis, Amra, Enis, his friend, and me hanging out in Anis's small apartment. It was a frosty night, still without heat and running water. We were sitting around the table, a candle lit, and in the absence of any sort of entertainment, Anis played guitar, and we were all singing. When we became hungry, Enis suggested his friend make a pizza.

"She makes something out of nothing," he said.

His friend seemed to be a bit on a wild side. Her long blond hair was all crazy, as if she had been electrocuted. She had thick glasses and wore a mismatched colorful skirt with a blouse on top. She ended up making a pizza over the gas stove, and we all finished it in a matter of minutes. When time came to sleep, as the curfew had already settled in, we decided Enis, his friend, and I would sleep in the same bed. I insisted on sleeping in the middle, between Enis and his friend. Was it to keep me warm during the chilly night? Was I sensing some jealousy in their interactions? Was it purely for logistical purposes? I did not know.

A few weeks had passed, and I was all alone in Anis's apartment. I often hid there from my parents to smoke a cigarette and have some alone time. Suddenly, the phone rang, and I answered the phone.

"Hello, is this Nadija?" There was a voice on the other end I could not recognize.

"Yes, this is she." I was still confused about to whom I had just responded.

"This is Enis. Nadija, I have a question for you. Do you love me?" I thought it was some kind of joke, so I went with it.

"Sure, I love you."

"Do you really?" I hesitated a bit at that point because I didn't know what his question meant or where it was heading.

"I guess I do." I didn't know what else to say. He had me stumped.

"I love you, too, Nadija. Marry me."

"Ummm. I have to go." I hung up, in obvious shock, as I finally realized that he was being serious.

Later, my mother told me that Enis called me from a mental institution. She advised me to stay away from him, even though he was most likely harmless. They said he had gone mental, and nobody was surprised, given his experience of seeing his father and brother die in front of his eyes.

I somehow learned that the night I slept in between him and his friend, he interpreted it as some kind of longing for him and a way to shelter him from different women, because I was his only and he mine. I felt sick to my stomach when I realized I had created a huge misunderstanding—a potential turmoil in his head that might have ushered him into a mental institution. And so, should I be more careful about expressing my feelings from here on? How do I distinguish genuine love from crazy obsession? Will I ever kiss a boy, or is that just a fantasy to be lived till the end of my life? Will I be kissing the right one?

I was exhausted and tired. The war seemed to have warped many things that once were normal. In the many instances, when the surprises and shocks of war took place, I would wonder where all this was going. Will the war ever end? What is going to happen to all of us? Will we survive the war? If so, how do we end the war? Are we going to have enough soldiers to defend us? Are there enough young Bosnian boys to enlist in the army to protect us?

This was the number one reason I couldn't care less about dating any longer. I had decided, consciously or not, to take a break from dating and live my life, day by day, as if it were the last one.

CHAPTER 18

The Wedding

Everyone, when there's war in the air, learns to live in a new element: falsehood.
—Jean Giraudoux

UNLIKE ME, Amra's interest in boys developed from an early age. Her puberty struck her suddenly and hard; her body sprouted like a wild blossom. She grew tall in a short amount of time, and her body curved like a windy road. Instead of focusing on school, her primary interests revolved around boys. Every time she had a boyfriend, I would get consumed by her relationship as if it were my own. After her date, she would come home and tell me all about it: what her boyfriend said, how they kissed, how they made out, what their next date plans were. All of it. She fell for boys fast. She was the person who fell in love easily and wanted her boyfriend to be her world. That's why the breakups were painful for her. On such occasions when we went to bed and she would recount repeatedly how her boyfriend broke up with her, what exactly he said, what might have led up to it, she would cry, and then I would cry as well.

Her relationship with Anis was more stable, even though their love began under the shells and bullets. Was it a testament of true love given the circumstances, or did the conditions hide something else? Everybody knew they were an item. My mom took in Anis as if he was her own son. When she cooked, she cooked for him as well. When she washed clothes, she offered to wash his. He felt like he was already part of our family. As we never met Anis's parents and younger sister, they were only stories to us, fruits of our imagination. Late at night, when tired of playing guitar, Anis would recount stories about his family describing each member. His mother was a hair stylist. After they escaped to Germany at the beginning of the war, she could find a job in a hair salon. His father now worked as a construction worker, something he had never done before, in order for the family to survive in diaspora. His sister was still in high school and lived with a boyfriend from Bijeljina, a city in North Bosnia.

Amra and Anis seemed good together. He adored her and showed it by caressing her hair on top of her head while cooing to her like a baby. She loved his attention and reciprocated his love by giving him a hug or a kiss. For them, getting married never was a topic for discussion during the war. Amra was sixteen when she first met Anis, while he was twenty-two. Perhaps too young to tie the knot.

Eventually, getting married during the war became an ordinary occurrence, like putting socks on in the morning. It was no big deal. Many people we knew were getting married. People in their teens, early twenties, widowed, separated, people whose spouse left in the beginning of the war… it was an epidemic. Amra and Anis had friends, Lejla and Dado, a couple who got together during the war and got married, as it would make their lives easier. They were an odd couple to me, both in character and looks. She was short and plump, with a perfectly round face wrapped in her long hair and a darker complexion, and was always quick with a snappy comeback. Dado had beautiful blue eyes and, while not tall like most Bosnians, had a stature of confidence and a great sense of humor. He was someone you'd want to hang out with all the time. After they got married, Lejla immediately became pregnant and gave birth to a beautiful baby girl. They began pressuring Amra and Anis to do the same.

"You really should do it. It's great. We love being married and having a kid. Guaranteed, you will love it too."

When their baby turned one, Dado's father, a prominent lawyer with connections, found a convoy to get Lejla and their baby out of Sarajevo. They ended up finding their way to Saudi Arabia, where a new life awaited them, husbandless and fatherless. Dado stayed behind to serve in the army. He came over to Anis's apartment to tell us how things went as Lejla and the baby were departing.

He took the cigarette out of his mouth and exhaled smoke, took a brief pause, and said, "As they were leaving, tears were falling down my back." Interestingly, this is something one would say sarcastically when they mean the exact opposite. Anis and I looked at each other and didn't know how to react. Is he serious or is he joking? Why would he cry, after all? His wife and baby would be safe and no longer needed to worry about survival, barely existing. But when Dado heard from Lejla on rare occasions, the message was often that she wanted to come back. Her life was harder than it was before. But it was too late. There was no coming back into the siege of Sarajevo.

On September 12, 1994, Amra turned nineteen. Shortly before, Anis and Amra decided they would marry. Indeed, they wouldn't run into the separation anxiety scenario that Lejla and Dado did, because Amra had no place to go. They would stay together no matter what.

People in the former Yugoslavia upheld long marriages, proud and strong. Getting a divorce was an anomaly and was guaranteed to lead to a poor reputation for all family members. It was a sacred bond that, in most cases, would last a lifetime. We all envisioned this bond for Amra and Anis. They set the date for their marriage to be September 17, 1994. When Anis's parents heard of this news, they sent a package with food and a wardrobe for Amra and Anis. The chances of finding a wedding dress in Sarajevo were quite slim. They sent her a beige two-piece suit and matching color heels. They sent me a mini dress with small flower prints.

Preparations for the wedding took place immediately. Amra and Anis went downtown and found an open jewelry store that sold wedding bands. My mother and our old neighbor, Devla, prepared food the day before. My mom was crafty and made dishes from whatever food she could get her hands on.

As was the case with most weddings in Bosnia, the groom and bride were followed by a line of cars toward the New Sarajevo City Hall where the ceremony took place.

Before they left the apartment, Devla threw water on the ground outside our front door for good luck. My mother asked her not to use too much; carrying water up the stairs was hard enough. As the cars lined up, the drivers honked as it was a custom. Some people pulled out their pistols and fired a few shots into the sky from their cars. Upon arrival, everyone in the wedding party surrounded the bride and the groom. When I saw them in the center, I looked at them more closely. They were so happy, but Amra had some more growing up to do. Her baby face was soft, with the smile of an innocent child. Her teeth were sticking out, as she refused to wear braces as a young child. She looked a bit lost, confused, shy even. Anis seemed more confident, laughing at the jokes the groom often becomes subjected to. They were both skinny and food deprived, but love would compensate for that which was lost, all that was out of reach during the war.

The ceremony did not last long. My cousin Dženana and Anis's cousin Kenan served as their witnesses. Shortly after, we headed back home, where my parents were waiting to greet the newly wedded couple. The living and dining rooms were set up with tables covered with white linens and food. My parents waited proudly, taking turns on getting congratulatory wishes from the guests. Around thirty people showed up, mostly family members and Amra's and Anis's friends. By then, Dado came back into my life strictly as a platonic friend. He had been dating a model who lived in Dobrinja. We invited him because he had a video camera to tape the ceremony and reception.

The power was shut that night, and we couldn't play music through the stereo. When darkness fell, we lit candles. My parents hired a professional accordion player. As the folk music played and people sang with their flat voices, laughter broke out once in a while. I watched the faces in the flickering candles and witnessed a collective pile of sadness. There was deep and unpalpable sense of absence of many things that were once joyful and happy. As the accordion was delivering sad notes, it suddenly hit me: my sister is married now. I felt like I had lost her forever. No more sharing secrets with each other, no more sharing the room, no more talking to each other endlessly about many things or making fun of people in our childish and silly ways. Someone asked me when I was going to get married.

I shrugged and, with pride, answered, "No way until I finish college."

As the night was ending, Amra and Anis headed down to Anis's apartment that now suddenly represented many things: the place for their honeymoon, their new sanctuary, and the space that stole my sister away from me forever.

CHAPTER 19

∽

Volleyball

$\mathcal{W}$ ar is cruelty, and none can make it gentle.
—Gilbert Parker

IN JANUARY 1995, Jasmina and I heard that a local radio station was organizing a big rock and roll concert named Rock Under Siege. The concert would take place on January 14, and more than a dozen local bands would perform. Sloga, located a block from the main street of Sarajevo, was the chosen venue, big enough for a couple thousand people. Jasmina and I somehow got a hold of tickets. We soon discovered that the police lifted the curfew on the night of the concert, making the event a big deal.

Before the war, Jasmina and I were just getting into the music scene. We had attended a couple of major concerts in 1991, featuring famous Yugoslav bands. One concert, Yutel for Peace, was meant to protest wars in the Balkans and brought in many famous musicians. Like all other calls for peace, that concert was fruitless.

Rock Under Siege happened on a chilly night. Our friends Miki and Miro showed up with a bottle of vodka. We passed it around and sipped in front of Sloga, hoping to keep us warm. The night seemed surreal. Band after band, the energy in Sloga was rising within the mosh pit near the stage. People were in a trance as if being held by a thousand little angels, carried into a better world. Our happiness ran wild, as it felt peace might have been around the corner.

Until February 5. Sometime around noon, the breaking news was announced that a mortar shell had killed over sixty people and wounded more than a hundred at the Markale market in the heart of the city. It was a dreadful day when everyone felt there was no end in sight, and more fear of the unknown settled in. Just when people were feeling more comfortable and congregate in public places, trying to live a normal life again, the enemy took advantage of the crowds and attacked. Who died? Do we know anyone? Any children? My mother was cursing the enemy all the time and wishing the worst on them. She couldn't help it. She was angry and hopeless. She cried, and her skinny self would curl into a ball at night and stay silent until falling asleep.

But people had to learn to move on from these atrocities. We went out again with no hesitation. We walked on the streets; we attended house parties; we met up with our friends; we went out to fetch water; we went to the salon to get a haircut, and we went to school every day despite the chaos.

My classes moved from the basement of my building to what used to be a store during peacetime in Dobrinja Three. The Soros Foundation donated money to the Sarajevo school system, so that textbooks were published and printed, and studying supplies, such as pencils and notebooks, were delivered to the students. Selma, Enisa, Faruk, and I coordinated our departure from Dobrinja Five so we could walk to school together. Our teachers took our education more seriously—whether the location made any difference, I wasn't sure. But I immersed myself into subject matters more seriously, because my teachers had little sympathy for those unprepared for class. My biology teacher was demanding. Her lectures were interesting and clear, but you had to pay close attention. My math professor was my mother's friend from high school, so I had a bit of leeway with grades—having connections made one's life easier—but my grades were still below average, as I had no affinity for the hard sciences. But you often received passing grades for character if not merit. When she lectured, though, she would often scare the crap out of me.

When teaching geometry, she would say, "*Na dija-gramu...*" She made it sound like she was calling on me to answer a question, but all she was saying, in translation, was "On diagram." When I told Jasmina, she laughed so hard and told our friends, who also found it funny.

I tried to be an excellent student, but I didn't feel my brain was functioning properly. As a student of Gimnazija, which was more difficult than the trade high school, I had to study Bosnian, English, German, and Latin—all the subjects which I ultimately had a difficult time grasping. Well, maybe I didn't have an affinity for languages either? Geography was my favorite class, held by a young teacher who had extremely high expectations for us. She had long curly hair and big blue eyes, often wearing her long leather coat, looking tough when she posed a question. As was often the case in the former Yugoslavia, teachers would tell you to stand in front of the map hung on the wall facing the students and ask the student to identify different locations on the map. Show me the Alps. Show me the Danube River. Where does it start? Where does it end? I would, with pride, answer all her questions quickly, but she still ended up giving me a B. She was a tough cookie.

On occasion, I would fiercely argue with one of my teachers. Our history professor—a bald man at the top of his head with long hair on the sides, one side combed all the way to the other, and an accent from out of town—lectured on what historically began wars. In my ignorance, I began telling him that *papak* started the war in Bosnia. The term *papak* was derogatory for someone who grew up in a village, often uneducated, and moved to a city thinking he or she is emancipated and belonged there. They usually take over and change the rules and stir up dissonance among those who were well educated. Of course, I was wrong. The discussion became heated, and he was raising his voice to get his point across. But I argued back, with a bit of a sarcastic tone in my voice, somewhat amused by his reaction.

I wasn't so surprised I didn't excel at school. All the new subjects overwhelmed me, and even more so the circumstances under which I had to study. The power still went on only at certain times, and if it wasn't on, I would have to study under candlelight, which strained my eyes and gave me a headache. I was often hungry and couldn't concentrate on what I was reading. In the winter, my hands were often too cold to hold my textbook. For some students in my class, school appeared to be easy. My class had a few geniuses whom I deeply admired and was afraid to talk to in fear they would proclaim me unfit for the school. But I carried on doing my best and passed.

In 1994, local bars in the city began opening. A particular club called Obala was open all night, and you'd often need to pull an all-nighter to avoid curfew. The club would brim with cigarette smoke, but it was a fun venue Jasmina and I liked to hang out in. The spirit was such that everyone was friendly and made you feel you belonged. But I yearned for healthier places to feel the belonging. Drinking and partying were taking a toll on me, as I felt alcohol's affect.

At school, I heard that a volleyball club was being formed, and the coach was looking for girls to join. My neighbor and classmate, Enisa, had played volleyball in the past and one day told me, "Nadija, you'd be a perfect candidate for volleyball. You're tall. You should join the club."

So I did. Our coach was a woman in her thirties, Sevda, with big teeth that didn't look like they belonged in her small head. She had neck-length curly hair with highlights and was on the shorter side for a volleyball coach. We met in front of her building one day, and the girls gathered around her while she laid down the rules and shared the practice schedule. During summer, we'd train twice a week on the court in Dobrinja Three, right behind Dado's building. In the beginning, she taught us how to pass the ball back and forth, bending down our knees and how to hit the ball while standing up. She taught us how to serve, how to gain precision when serving the ball, and add strength to the serve. Enisa had a killer serve. When she touched the ball, those on the other side of the court ducked to protect themselves.

I loved playing volleyball. My mother encouraged me to go to every training session. Enisa would wait for me in front of the building, and we'd go together. At the beginning of each session, we would warm up and jump in the air like kangaroos. Sevda always screamed as to motivate us: "Jump, jump, jump, higher, higher!" She wanted us to gain height above the net so we could spike better. Sevda often told us that if we kept up with practice, we could end up looking like models. Lean and strong.

Even though I loved the sport, I never rose to the top. I never was the best on the team. I was unusually self-conscious when I played, and I worried about being watched by passerby or boys standing near the court. When we practiced, my eyes often gazed at Dado's window to see if he might be secretly watching me and perhaps admiring my moves or devotion to the sport.

A few months passed, and Sevda announced that our first tournament would take place in Hrasnica. The place was on the other side of the airport. The entire team would go. She already had a strong lineup in mind, which I wasn't part of. Enisa was our strongest player and the team captain. Jadranka and Dajana were the next best.

Sevda told us they had found a few families in the neighborhood who would take us in for a couple of days. I would stay with another girl from the team. When I heard about this, I didn't know how we would get there. The city was still under siege, and there was no way to avoid enemy lines if we were to take a normal route to Hrasnica. The same day I learned about the secret that the army had kept from civilians. A tunnel under the airport runway was dug from Dobrinja to Hrasnica back in 1993. We got the instructions to meet at the school on the day of our departure before we headed over to the tunnel by foot.

The Bosnian Army regulated the tunnel, and they controlled traffic between the two ends. If you were claustrophobic, you wouldn't fare well. The tunnel was narrow and short and muddy. Whoever was leading the way had a flashlight, so we could see what was in our path. I had my backpack on, and I had to duck a few times to avoid collision with the ceiling. The trip seemed quite long, even though the tunnel was less than a kilometer. The air was entombed in the narrow walls surrounded by mud, so it was difficult to breathe. I would have tried to walk faster to end this painful journey, but I couldn't pass anybody in front of me. Finally, the daylight was slowly beginning to emerge until we stepped outside onto free land.

I turned around and saw Dobrinja and my old neighborhood. Sadness came over me as I was reminded how unfortunate it was for the people of Sarajevo to be trapped in a city full of suffering. Hrasnica was another world. Sarajevo still occasionally got shelled and bullets were constantly heard, but Hrasnica appeared as if barely any hardship was felt. The people looked different, somewhat happy, and they smiled.

We arrived at our host family's house near the school where the tournament was held. They took us to our room, which was dark and uninviting. I didn't want to stay there longer than I had to, so I asked Aida, my teammate, if she wanted to walk around the neighborhood.

Aida was a punk rock chick who wore Dr. Martens boots year-round and had no trouble talking to strangers. She and I were the only ones who smoked, but we hid it from Sevda for the fear she would scream at us if she saw us smoking. We found a bench in a park and sat down to watch people walk by. Aida was searching for someone to ask for a cigarette. She finally stopped a young man, with a mustache and beard and a trench coat on, and asked him for one.

"Here." He pulled out a pack and offered one to both of us. "Where are you girls from?" When we told him, he said, "Oh, wow. Dobrinja? That must be rough. What are you doing here?"

"Volleyball tournament."

"I'm having a party at my place tonight, so if you girls are up to it, come." He wrote his address on a piece of paper and handed it to Aida.

Later on that day, we played in a tournament. I sat on the bench the whole time and watched my team struggle for points. Sevda would switch players once in a while, but she never picked me. She would walk up and down the court and scream, "Come on, girls! Come on, spike it now, now!"

We lost all the games but one. It was a disappointing defeat, but it was understandable considering we played against more experienced teams that had trained under normal circumstances.

We were sent to our respective host homes and were told not to go anywhere. The tournament would continue the following day, and the girls should take a much-needed rest. We all went to bed at a reasonable time.

Shortly after, someone knocked on our room window, and I heard someone whisper, "Nadija, Nadija." Who could it be? I peeked through the window and outside stood Aida, all excited as if she just had discovered another planet. "Nadija, let's go! Let's go to the party! I'll wait for you here."

I turned around to see what my roommate was up to, but she was extremely quiet and appeared to be in a deep sleep. I couldn't tell her our secret.

"Let me change first and I'll meet you outside," I told her.

We found ourselves on the streets of Hrasnica, looking for the address of the bearded guy we had met earlier that day. The night was still young, and we had enough time to go to the party, go back to the room, and get enough sleep. We finally found his place, but as we approached, we didn't hear noise or music coming from behind the door. We knocked on the door twice until he finally opened it. He was alone. The party that he promised wasn't happening, but he told us to come in any way. Aida and I looked at each other, shrugged our shoulders, and entered his apartment.

We sat in the kitchen and began exchanging niceties. He asked how our games went while he was offering us cigarettes. He pulled a bottle of *rakija*, 60 percent proof alcohol, out of his kitchen cabinet and three shot glasses. We all sat on the couch with him in the middle. As we got tipsy, we began to laugh and make jokes.

After a while, he stood up and said, "I'm hungry. I need to fix something to eat."

He opened his refrigerator, and the miracle happened: he pulled an egg. Two eggs!

My eyes widened, and I screamed, "Are those real?"

I had not seen an egg in years, not to mention eaten one. He scrambled both, and Aida and I savored every bite. The taste barely resembled the powdered eggs we ate since the beginning of the war. I couldn't wait to tell my family and friends that I ate an egg. I was sure they'd be excited for me.

The next thing we knew, it was past the curfew. When we realized this, our host offered us to stay at his place, but we knew it would look bad when our teammates woke up in the morning and saw the two of us missing. We took the risk and walk back to our host homes during curfew. We said our goodbyes, thanked him for sharing his eggs a million times again, and found our way back. It was a short walk, during which we didn't run into a single soul. When I arrived, I changed quickly into my pajamas and slipped into the sheets. All was well.

The following day, Aida and I pretended as if nothing had happened. We arrived at the school for the remaining tournament games, just like Sevda instructed us. I ended up on the bench the whole time again, but that was all right with me since I felt hungover from *rakija*. I didn't think I could even jump. We lost the games again, and we lost the tournament. We packed our bags and went back home through the tunnel. As I was entering the tunnel, I thought, How close yet so far away from freedom? It was a strange feeling to realize that only a narrow tunnel separated me from being free. But I couldn't stay even if I wanted to. I had to go back to the siege and my family.

Somehow, the trip back through the tunnel seemed shorter and easier since I was prepared for the journey.

A couple of days later, I found out that someone had ratted me out. As I was told later, when Sevda found out, she was so pissed that she began screaming, "That's a disgrace to my team! She risked her life, how dare she!" She kicked me off the team. She didn't even think twice. She had asked Enisa to tell me I was no longer part of the club. My heart sank when I found out. I knew I would never be the best, but I found so much psychological relief in playing the sport and being physical. It took me to a place where I felt alive—a place that gave me strength.

Aida swore she hadn't told her, but I thought she had. I realized it must have been my roommate, who probably deserved an Oscar for pretending so well to be sleeping that night. I didn't know what benefit she had in telling Sevda that I had left the room.

I told Enisa in secrecy that Aida went with me and begged her not to tell Sevda. If I was kicked out, so be it! There was no need for two people getting punished. Soon after, Sevda found out that Aida had been my partner in crime. Instead of kicking her out, she had Enisa let me know I could rejoin the club and we would all forget about what had happened. But by then, I had accepted the loss and moved on from volleyball. Enisa tried to convince me I was making a mistake, but I was determined to stick to my gun.

CHAPTER 20

The Beginning of the End

*W*ar settles nothing.
—Dwight D. Eisenhower

SERBS MUST HAVE FELT desperate about the status quo of the city, so they shelled us heavily in the spring of 1995. The school was closed during shelling and rescheduled for later dates to make up for the lost time. We heard that the Bosnian Army, along with the Croatian Army, began pushing the enemy lines and reoccupying land that once had belonged to Muslims and Croats. Because of this, the local Serbs in Sarajevo were so frustrated and demoralized by their losses that they shelled us more frequently and intensely.

By then, Amra was pregnant, and her stomach was growing so fast, as if she ate yeast every day. With nothing else to do during the day, she carefully outlined what nutrients would keep a pregnant woman healthy and feed her baby, notes she read from the book borrowed from our neighbor. She wrote:

Daily needs of an average pregnant woman (aged 20-33), height 160 cm, weight around 65 kg:

- *Calories: 2750*
- *Iron: 15 mgr*
- *Protein: 95 gr*
- *Fat: 50 gr*
- *Calcium: 1,5 gr*
- *Phosphorus: 1 gr*
- *Flor: 1 mg*
- *Vitamin A: 6000 IJ*
- *Vitamin C: 40 mgr*
- *Vitamin D: 600 IJ*
- *Folic acid: 0,8 mgr*

Her list seemed more like a far-fetched dream, something you'd read in a sci-fi book. Her appetite was growing at an extraordinary rate. She ate a whole loaf of bread in one sitting. My mother made her a simple spinach dish from our garden, and she mixed it with water, powdered eggs, and milk. It was the healthiest meal for a pregnant woman during the war. When shells fell near the building, Amra and her enormous belly would jump off the couch, and she would roll down the carpet like a barrel. During her pregnancy, Amra smoked the entire time. Anis, Amra, and I went to the hospital one day for a regular ultrasound checkup, during which her doctor told her that her placenta was black. Even though the placenta filtered a lot of the harmful things out of the baby's food, the doctor advised her to cut down on smoking.

When we walked outside the hospital, I was angry. "You really should quit smoking. I don't know what you're thinking, seriously."

Amra stared at the ground without saying a word, while Anis interjected with his own sense of humor. "Oh, relax. Here, take one. You'll feel better."

He took a pack of cigarettes out of his pocket, offered one to Amra, and laughed.

No matter what smoking might do to her baby, Amra continued to smoke. Her lips and her feet swelled; she looked like Buddha with pale skin and a short spiky haircut. Her enormous belly posed her difficulty moving around and doing simple chores around the house. When she washed her clothes in the bathroom, she would sit on a plastic stool in front of the bathtub, take off all her clothes, except her undies and bra, and dig into the big bucket while cussing. The days were hot, and she sweated profusely.

I was happy that I would have a niece. The baby was due mid-September, and the day couldn't come fast enough.

Because the front lines became belligerent everywhere in the country, the soldiers from different regions were deployed to areas where the land was taken back from the Serbs most successfully. Selma and I were getting sick of the situation, and we wanted to join the army to go fight.

I saw myself in the trenches with the other soldiers, with a gun in my hands, waiting for the enemy to appear so I could defend myself, my family, and all the innocent people in the neighborhood. I pictured myself wearing the uniform, army boots, and carrying a gun on my shoulder. After a long day in battle, I'd stop by the barbershop and shoot the crap with Huso. You had lots of customers today? Yeah? It was busy? Oh no, don't worry. I don't need to go first. I can wait. I just need my hair washed, that's all. It got nasty from all the dirt in the trenches. And I could go to the army kitchen, a forbidden area for civilians, and have my lunch while hanging out with the boys. I was obsessed with being a soldier and wanting to make a difference. I wanted to stop the war.

When we told Muhamed, the army commander, that we wanted to join the army, grab a gun, and fight, he laughed at us.

"You couldn't even carry a gun. And look at the tiny Selma. She'd fall over if she put one on her shoulder."

We pleaded with him, but he didn't want to hear it.

At the beginning of July, the news reported that Srebrenica, a town in East Bosnia, had been occupied by Serbs. The town was protected by Dutch troops and considered a 'safe haven.' The Serbs had taken most of the towns surrounding Srebrenica, and they expelled or killed thousands of Muslims. An ethnical cleansing at its best. The Muslim population that lived in Srebrenica before the war congregated in Potočari, a relatively small space where they cohabited with the Dutch troops. One morning, the Dutch troops let the Serb soldiers enter the safe haven. When my parents heard of this news, they were shaken. I didn't even know a safe haven could exist. For me, nothing and nowhere was safe. Later, it was discovered that the Serbs had killed thousands of Muslim men and boys in two days, creating mass graves where they left their bodies and covered them with dirt. The women —their wives, mothers, sisters, daughters—were raped and killed, and many were taken to concentration camps. When the news spread, my parents' hope plunged. They were growing more concerned that perhaps, someday, the siege we had been under for over three years would end the same. Sarajevo would be occupied, and we'd all be killed. Like flies. Perhaps the recent intense shelling in Sarajevo was better explained after this news.

Anis heard his brigade would be deployed to another part of the country soon. Many Dobrinja soldiers would be deployed to different regions, and many didn't return. Anis didn't want to go, and he most definitely didn't want to leave his newly married wife and unborn child. He tried to come up with a plan to avoid going, but however he sliced it, he couldn't avoid the army orders.

I went downstairs to Amra's and Anis's apartment one day and shortly after, our cousin Emir arrived. He entered the apartment like a torpedo, and he turned to Anis, rubbing his palms, and said, "So you really wanna do this?"

"I don't see any other way."

"How are we gonna do this?"

I stood there, clearly not understanding what was going on. "I'm going to kneel on the floor and put my foot on the tabletop, and then you come onto my leg with full force."

A few seconds later, once Anis was in position, Emir jumped on his leg with as much force as he could muster.

"Ahhhhhhhhhhhhhhhhhhhhhh!" Anis screamed. Emir grabbed his

stomach and laughed. I clenched my teeth and felt Anis's pain. This couldn't be easy.

"Did I break it?" Emir couldn't stop laughing.

"No, I don't think so. You'll have to do it again."

Same steps again and again. Every time Emir repeated the landings, the louder Anis screamed. We heard a snap when Emir finally broke Anis's leg. The scream and the pain were ones you wouldn't wish upon your worst enemy.

"Hey, I have to go now. You're all set, right?"

Anis could barely talk. He grabbed his leg and lied down on the floor for a long time.

The outcome was exactly what Anis had planned. He went to the ER and told the doctor that he had fallen down the stairs and hurt his leg. His doctor told him he needed a cast and crutches. The doctor excused him from the Army for three weeks. We all swore on our mother and everything precious to us we wouldn't tell anyone how Anis got out of being deployed to the front lines. Had the Army discovered what he did, he would have ended up in jail for a long time.

It turned out well that Anis was excused. The Serbs shelled us relentlessly and constantly. It reminded us of the beginning of the war, when we were just learning about different types and sizes of shells and bullets. The only difference was that now, we all seemed to be experts in identifying both.

By the end of August, the days were pretty hot and steamy. By then, we had gotten used to being able to walk around during a break from constant shelling. Like in the beginning of the war, we were again advised not to go outside because shells could fall any time.

On August 28, the enemy struck and launched a mortar into the Markale market in downtown again. This time, it killed over forty and wounded over seventy people. I sensed a lot of fear in my parents, as they could not see the ending in sight.

With these recent developments, my mom couldn't go to work, and we didn't go to school. Some soldiers were advising us to be patient. A lot of the land was being captured back from the Serbs, and the Bosnian Army was steadily advancing, penetrating enemy lines everywhere around the country. Possibly, the war could end soon if the Army kept up its success.

Two days after the Markale massacre, we all sat in the living room, and someone said, "Are those planes?"

During the war, planes in the sky became a foreign concept. The engine sounded loud, flying above us, signaling a forthcoming change. We began feeling unsettled, as we didn't know what these planes were doing and to whom they belonged. Somebody said, "Hey, look, they're dropping bombs!"

After the bombs fell on the ground, the smoke was coming out of the hills that surrounded Sarajevo. Those planes belonged to NATO, and those bombs were destroying Serbian artillery on the hills surrounding Sarajevo. When we realized what was happening, we all started to cheer and jump up and down in the living room. Freedom at last! No more shelling of the innocent citizens of Sarajevo. All the hope I had smiled down on me again, and I began feeling relief. The end of the siege, it seemed, just knocked on our door. It was August 30, and it was my mom's birthday—she received the best birthday gift ever.

Soon thereafter, the shelling completely ceased. People could walk freely. We no longer held fear about suddenly being knocked to the ground and hurt by shrapnel. Cars on the street multiplied suddenly, like bees coming out of their hives. Over the time, I had become numb to gunfire shells and powerful explosions. My senses, confused and conditioned in a certain war way, shifted slowly. When a car drove by one day, I ducked under the table as fast as I could and began shaking. My heart was beating fast. The sounds of the lightning and thunder were often mistaken for shooting, and we'd cringe when this scary gift of nature arrived.

The timing of the NATO rescue could not be any better. Shortly after, around midnight, Amra began feeling cramps in her stomach. Her water broke. By then, Anis returned to his Army duties and was on his night patrol shift. Amra stayed over at our parents' place for this reason. She woke all of us up and told us she needed to go to the hospital right away. My mother called Sabaheta and asked her to come along.

The night was calm. The sky was filled with stars clearly seen without light pollution. My mother, Amra, and Sabaheta met in front of our building and headed to the main street to hitchhike for a ride to the hospital. We didn't have a car, so I watched the three of them standing along the main street and waiting for a car to appear. The moon was shining full and bright that I could clearly see them fidgeting around. They stood there for a good ten minutes until a car finally showed. All three stuck their thumb out, and the car stopped instantly. Amra and Sabaheta entered the car that quickly disappeared down the moonlit street while my mother remained standing on the street and excitedly waving to the speeding car.

The birth of my niece was quick. She was born into the world, healthy and plump. When you looked at her, you'd never think she was conceived amid a war. She looked exactly like her mother when she was a baby—round red cheeks and eyes like a Chinese doll. When Amra was pregnant, she had a dream of a woman coming to her and telling her, "Name your child Dženana." Amra thought it must have been some weird dream every woman had during her pregnancy. Ifeta, our neighbor, told her it was a sign of luck and that she had to honor the dream. When my niece was born, it was a no-brainer that she would be named Dženana.

The following day, all of us headed to the hospital to pick up Amra and the baby. The Bosnian tradition is to have a designated person carry the newborn out of the hospital. It is a special moment for the chosen person. That person was going to be me.

When we arrived, Amra looked as if someone had beaten her all night. She looked pale and exhausted. When she mustered her strength, she turned to us and whispered, "There was a woman on the bed next to me. When she gave birth to her child, she kept telling the doctor she didn't want the child."

"So what happened to the child?"

"Not sure. My guess is they took the baby for adoption somewhere."

A lot of similar stories during the war circled around. Women who ended up pregnant could not have an abortion and ended up abandoning their baby.

I couldn't wait to hold Dženana in my hands. The nurse came over to tell us we could pick up the baby. She took Dženana out of the room where cribs were lined up behind a large window, and in each lied a crying baby. Dženana was wrapped up in a white blanket, looking like a loaf of bread.

The nurse came out, and she asked Anis and me, "And who are you?"

"I'm the father," Anis said.

"And I'm the aunt. I'll take her."

Dženana got passed over to me like a torch at the Olympic Games. She was asleep. She was beautiful. I walked carefully so as not to stumble and drop her on the floor.

When we arrived home, my mother unwrapped Dženana for inspections: two legs, ten toes, two arms, ten fingers, everything perfect and in one piece. She changed her quickly and wrapped her again in white. She laid her on the couch to make baby sounds. I leaned over to examine her one more time, and I realized how beautiful she was in all her innocence. Her life marked the beginning of something beautiful—growth, love, and a spring of hope.

CHAPTER 21

❧

The Ending

*O*nly the dead have seen the end of the war.
—George Santayana

WITH THE END of the war, we looked at our future in a better light. Or was it simply an immense sense of relief? We simply knew: no more sudden dying on the streets, no more bullets flying, no more shells falling in random places, no more lack of running water, no more power shutoffs, no more being cold and hungry. Peace felt good. But now what? What would happen to our home that had been taken by the enemy three and a half years ago? We were wondering about what had happened to the people we once knew. Did they survive the war? Did they escape to other parts of the globe? What about those who were captured and sent to concentration camps? Connection to most people had been lost. We were slowly finding out about who had become our enemy and who a true victim of this war was.

Some of my parents' Serb friends fled to the other side at the brink of the war, automatically becoming our new enemy. My parents, even as adults, couldn't understand how these people could turn against us in a matter of days. Before the war, my mother often visited with her Serb colleague and friend, Nevenka, who lived in our neighborhood. She was tall and slim with deep dark hair, my only memory of her. Now, my mother couldn't comprehend that Nevenka ever held such a deeply rooted hatred for Muslims that facilitated the disintegration of their long-lived friendship in a matter of days. After Nevenka suddenly disappeared, my mother would often wonder where she might be and tried to guess that she was in Pale, the Serb epicenter near Sarajevo, as she recalled that Nevenka's brother lived there before the war. I felt my mother's hurt by Nevenka's sudden disappearance she considered betrayal.

Growing up as a shy kid, I didn't get close to many people. My friend Svjetlana, who grew up across the street from me, came from a Serbian family and moved to Dobrinja Four a couple of years before the war. Last time I had seen Svjetlana was several days before she moved. We took a walk behind my building on a nice sunny day. Her face was plump, cheeks big as a house, from the medication she was taking. She'd tell me even though she was diagnosed with lupus, she was doing fine. Lupus meant "wolf" in Latin, she said. She'd say patients with lupus died from their kidneys giving out, but her kidneys were fine and she felt good and strong. I felt relieved by this discovery. After she moved, we exchanged a few letters until I never got a response from her on my last letter.

Shortly after, the wolf took her life. Her kidneys gave out. It was a hot August day when I learned about her death; I was on school break with nothing better to do, so I called up my school friend Olivera, announced "Svjetlana died!" and hung up the phone. I cried uncontrollably, finding her mortality surreal. A couple of weeks later, as a reaction to the shock, I had my first period.

My parents went to Dobrinja Four to visit Svjetlana's parents, as it was a custom in former Yugoslavia. As my mother recalled when she arrived home later, they all sat in the living room sectional, crying and mourning the much too premature death of my good friend. Even though political unrest was brewing in the country, and Svjetlana's parents must have known what was to come, there was no word of this during the visit. It didn't matter that my parents were Muslim, and Svjetlana's Serbs. A streak of humanity, something deeply felt, was shared by all in the room. I had no one to betray me. My only close Serbian friend was already six feet under. I made new friends during the war who came from Serbian or Croatian families or those from mixed marriages, and this was why this war made no sense to me. As for my parents, they still had many other friends they cherished.

Our neighbor from across the street in our old neighborhood, Biba, often came to visit us in our new home. She was married to a man who was a professional barber, Iso, and they stayed behind the day the enemy captured our neighborhood. Biba ended up in a concentration camp with other women and later released. Biba and Iso didn't have children, but they treated other children in our neighborhood as their own. Before the war, my parents used to go to their place for all-night parties where music and drinking were involved.

Iso was one of the friendliest neighbors around; he liked to hike the surrounding mountains before the war and was extremely active. It showed by how he carried himself when he walked. He looked strong and vital, always seemed to have been in a great mood, and was ready to exchange niceties. Biba was quiet and sweet. She had a mullet as long as I had known her, and it somehow seemed to have fit her well-rounded face and blue eyes.

When she came to visit us, she always carried a bagful of her personal items. She developed this habit after the Serbs occupied the old neighborhood, in case she had to escape from the enemy again. Her life was in that bag, and she did not travel without it.

When we spoke about Iso, she would tell us she didn't know what exactly happened to him the morning the Serbs captured him. But she felt deep inside that he was still alive. If you knew Biba before the war, quiet and sweet, you would be surprised at how convincingly and strongly she spoke up.

"I am a hundred percent sure he is still alive. I just feel it. You will see he will show up one day."

Sure enough, Iso was still alive. The morning the Serbs captured our neighborhood, Iso hid in the attic of their building. The neighborhood became a ghost town, with its only residents being the Serbian soldiers on duty, keeping the line between them and us. Iso lived in the attic, taking trips to his apartment whenever he could without being discovered. When the water from the faucet had been shut off and when all the sources were depleted, he peed in a cup and drank his own pee. He attempted to escape several times. But if a Serbian soldier didn't discover him, a Bosnian soldier might, thinking he was a Serbian soldier trying to cross to the Bosnian side and killing him.

No one knew how it happened, but after forty days of hiding in the attic, a Serbian soldier discovered Iso discovered while on a hunt for food. I imagine the soldier must have been surprised to find the sole individual in the empty land living with the ghosts. The day he was discovered, the Serbian soldiers beat him badly until he lay bleeding on the street. Instead of killing him, they chose another option and took him to the concentration camp in Kula near the airport. There, they put him to work as a barber, which he did for the rest of the war.

He was finally released as the war ended. There was a hostage exchange program between both sides. When we saw him, he looked beaten down, with scars covering his face and body. He seemed frightened, lifeless, as if someone had reached into his chest and removed his soul. He told us how he had escaped death three times, but as luck would have it, he was still alive. Biba and Iso organized a festive celebration for his survival my parents attended. They said Iso caught a rabbit and prepared it as a feast.

Gradually, we were discovering more and more about who had been killed during the enemy occupation of our neighborhood. On June 17, 1992, seventy-four people were killed on the spot. We later learned that the paramilitary *Orlovi* soldiers relied on a list of Muslims to kill on the spot that was provided by our Serb neighbors. Petra, our subdivision neighbor in the adjacent building, a single lady in her sixties, always seemed so nice and would give neighborhood children Easter eggs for the Orthodox Easter before the war. Every year, I looked forward to that day since Muslims didn't dye eggs and I found them adorable. But one day, she replaced her smile with an angry grimace and every time she saw us, she'd turn away or duck her head as if we didn't exist. I didn't understand why. Until we learned that Petra, among other Serb neighbors, helped put that kill list together. And if the information we received was correct, that meant my father was also on the list. I didn't and couldn't understand what we did to her to warrant the death of my innocent father. We heard other horror stories that the Serbian soldiers beheaded certain individuals and kicked their heads around like a soccer ball.

With all these stories slowly emerging, survival mode was wearing off and shut down. The realities of the war had settled in, and I finally felt like its true psychological impact.

The world had certainly gone mad during the war. We heard many stories about how people had gone insane while under siege. There was a man who ran up and down the streets of Sarajevo with a piece of lemon in his mouth, half naked. When asked why he was running all the time, his answer was, "If I didn't, I would go insane." Even police had become a danger to the public. When they stopped Mak Dizdar on the street after curfew, the same person who shared with Jasmina and I our very first beer, they beat him up, thinking that he had gone insane and used the famous poet's name. Were the streets not safe for different reasons now?

On the political front, things were looking up. The three presidents of Bosnia, Serbia, and Croatia agreed to the terms and conditions of the country that the US and Europe had helped design. The agreement was called the Dayton Agreement, as it was drafted in Dayton, Ohio, but later signed in Paris. The agreement would divide the country into two regions, whereby 51 percent would belong to the Bosnian Muslims and Croats. It was to be called the Federal Republic of Bosnia and Herzegovina, and it would comprise ten separate cantons, with Brčko included as an eleventh special canton. The remaining 49 percent would belong to the Orthodox Bosnian Serbs, and that part of the country would be called Republika Srpska. Although most people were happy that the war had finally ended, the arrangement made by the Dayton Agreement didn't favor most Bosnian Muslims. Some would say, "We would be better off if we kept fighting. We were gaining a lot of the land back."

Most people were content that they no longer had to worry about sudden death or a lack of necessities. It was strangely difficult to get used to running water or having electricity all the time. I expected losing either at any minute of the day. Open markets were filling with eggs, meat, milk, and fresh produce. When I tasted some of the food, I realized then how undernourished we were during the war.

Now that we had nothing to physically run and hide from and our survival mode was signaling the end, another internal battle had just begun. Our lives still promised many uncertainties. Did our newly formed freedom mean we could go anywhere around the country? While some immediate certainties were presented to us, many unknowns remained unanswered. Everything was up in the air, but the air felt clearer, and I was happy to breathe again.

The curfew in Sarajevo and other major Bosnian cities was still enforced but was lifted during religious holidays. Christmas in Sarajevo was not well celebrated, but the local cathedral would be open all night for visitors.

With a bottle of cognac in tow, Jasmina and I took advantage of the lifted curfew on Christmas Eve, and we headed downtown to savor the freedom of mobility. It was unusually cold that night, but as we sipped cognac, we felt warmer. The streets were bustling with people that night. Everyone wanted to feel the city that night like what it used to be before the war. I felt enlightened, as if I had been blind and could see again. We stopped by the cathedral, which was full of people, candles lit everywhere. The choir was singing carols, and it was an angelic experience. But it could have been also the fact that I was already feeling quite tipsy. Suddenly, Jasmina signaled me to come over to where she was standing. She pointed at the holy font, which looked as if someone had thrown up inside. To avoid bursting out laughing, we ran out of the cathedral and headed to our next stop.

By the time we got to KUK, we had consumed the bottle of cognac. We were visibly drunk, zigzagging on the street, and we continued to celebrate our freedom in friendly spirit. Someone handed us a couple of beers, and we continued to drink. It was already past midnight, maybe 4:00 a.m., and time to head back home. Before we headed downtown, Igor had offered the empty apartment of his parent's friends, where we would eventually crash that night. He said he would wait for us there, and all we had to do was knock on the door. The apartment was in the same building subdivision I lived, two floors down.

On our way home, we took the tram that was running all night for holiday celebrations. A rowdy group of three young men were laughing about something amusing. They seemed quite drunk themselves, which at that point made it easy for all of us to establish a connection. Jasmina recognized two of the men as band members. One was a bass player named Ogi, and another a singer in the band named D Throne. They played in the Rock Under Siege concert. The third man, with distinguished big blue eyes, was the bass player's best friend. His name was Zlatan.

"You two are from the band D Throne, right?" Jasmina asked. "Yes, we are."

"We came to the Rock Under Siege concert," we said proudly and began to sing and pretend like we were playing air guitar.

I was on the frontline yesterday
I was shot in the head

That was one of their songs, *Story from Sarajevo.*

"Were you really shot, or that's just the song?" the drunkenness in me retorted.

"Yeah, I was shot," Aris said. He was a guitar player and the singer of the band.

"Really?" I should have known better. Everything during the war was possible, but at that moment, I thought that being shot in the head equaled sudden death. "Show it."

He moved up the ponytail of his long hair and underneath, close to his ear, appeared a four- to five-centimeter scar.

"Oh, shit. Sorry, man. Are you doing all right now?" I said, regretting for doubting earlier.

"No worries."

They wanted to keep on talking, so we invited them to come along. The tram stop was a few kilometers from the apartment, so we walked through the night under the shiny moon.

When we arrived there, Igor was wide awake and ready to host. We played games until dawn. At one point, even though it was extremely cold, Jasmina and Ogi went outside on the balcony, where they seemed to have connected on a deeper level. When it was time for them to head home, we made plans to get together for New Year's Eve.

When I woke up the following day, I noticed red dots all over my face. What could it be? I figured it must have been all the alcohol I had consumed the night before. But strangely, my head was clear, and my anxiety subdued. The following day, when I had to take an oral exam in history, I was practically singing the answers. Everything I had read on the topic rolled off my tongue so easily, and I ended up getting a good grade.

Meanwhile, Jasmina was suddenly head over heels with Ogi. She was infatuated by him since the balcony experience. She seemed to have loved everything about him—his looks, his goofy sense of humor, his missing front tooth, but most of all, that he was a bass player, which she dreamed of becoming. We frequently hung out with Ogi and Zlatan, and they were becoming good friends. Ogi had the strangest stories to tell, like the one where his friend pooped in the bush and he snuck up behind him to steal his poop. When his friend stood up and turned around to examine the product of his relief, he was astonished to see that his poop was missing, and nothing was there. That was our new friend, Ogi. We adored him, and we enjoyed his and Zlatan's company.

CHAPTER 22

New Battle

War is the unfolding of miscalculations.
—Barbara W. Tuchman

THE NEWLY FOUND peace eventually proved as shell-shocking as the beginning of the war. We couldn't get used to it. I couldn't believe that a shell wouldn't fall suddenly or that people would no longer be dying from a bullet or shrapnel. We didn't believe that we could freely walk on the street, anywhere, and not worry about speeding up the pace to land at a safe destination as quickly as possible. Was the rain of shells really over? We could not believe that we were under normal circumstances again. People were now being held accountable for their actions and could no longer blame them on the war.

Instead of being happy and excited about the war ending, different feelings emerged—monstrous ones. I attributed those feelings to being lost and the fear of the unknown. My survival instinct ceased to guide me in a fast-paced chaos. A range of emotions was hitting me all day, every day. It was like my body had been charged during the entire war, and suddenly my nerves relaxed, and my body was perplexed by its new calm state.

At one time, I would have feelings of rage and often took it out on my parents. When I was ready to go out, they'd tell me not to stay late. And from the top of my lungs, I'd yell at them not to lecture me.

"Fuck off. Don't tell me what to do!"

How dare they discipline me now that I have survived the war? How dare they tell me what to do when I have my instincts that led me through the worst of times?

My mom would cry, as she didn't know what to do about my temper. Later, she'd stay quiet most of the time, as she might have feared my potential reactions. The rage in me was so strong that I had no way of controlling it. When Jasmina and I took a tram downtown on our way out one evening, a couple of kids were sitting behind us, and one of them began picking at the bottom of my long hair. Like a tornado approaching, my jaw clenched, my eyebrows came closer, and my voice finally gave in.

I screamed, from the top of my lungs, as I turned around and said, "Stop that crap!"

The kids behind me froze, didn't say a word, but naturally got the message that they should stop messing around with my hair. Jasmina laughed, but no one on the tram even blinked, as if my reaction was normal, something mild compared to the mayhem experienced prior.

When the rage inside was resting, depression came.

I was in the last year of high school, preparing to graduate in the spring of 1996. The teachers told us to buckle down and study hard so we would have an easier time getting into the college of our choice. I didn't know where I wanted to go or what I wanted to study. My future prospects were blurred. I lived day by day, trying to pass all my subjects.

I struggled. I did poorly in math. I could barely say a sentence in German. My conversational English was nonexistent, and almost the entire class flunked chemistry. For the Bosnian class, we had to read Steppenwolfe by Herman Hesse. Once I read it, I stayed up all night trying to figure out the meaning of it. I tossed and turned in bed, thinking about the book and trying to understand it. I was analyzing the main character's loneliness in society and his weird approach to life. But by dawn, I was so tangled up in my own theories that I had completely lost it. The following day, as suspected, my Bosnian teacher called my name and asked me to summarize the book and give my opinion. This oral exam was preclusive to the final grade. For a second, I felt brave and was about to tell the entire class about my brilliant literary discovery, but when I opened my mouth, I felt paralyzed. I'd point at the book with my fingers and begin with "In this book..." I'd drop the sentence like someone shut me off. I looked down in front of my desk and inside me, I prayed help would come from somewhere, and that I'd gather enough strength to continue. But there was nothing. Silence filled the room for a while, and it made the whole classroom feel uncomfortable.

I tried again: "In this book..."

I heard someone giggle. The teacher gave me at least five minutes to pull this off, but my fear was in a downward spiral and past the point of return.

The teacher finally gave up and said, "Nadija, it doesn't seem like you're ready today. Why don't we just continue some other time?"

I was embarrassed. Overcome by deep depression, I felt as if it took me by its claws, and I couldn't get out of its grasp.

On the plus side, I had my new niece, who had become the world I revolved around. She became everything to me, and I treated her as if I had given her birth. Amra, who was still getting used to being a mother and yelling at Dženana's bites while suckling her breast, had an unexplainable contempt for taking care of the child. When Dženana cried in the small room, my mother would advise Amra to go check up on her, and Amra's response was, "What? You want me to watch the child? Are you crazy?" Amra was only twenty, with her new world wrapped up in an immense responsibility—motherhood—that she was barely ready for.

When Dženana cried at night, I'd get up as soon as I heard her, pick her up, and take her to my bed to sleep with me. When I visited my friends during the day, I would take her in tow with me, and my friends and I would watch her crawl, salivate, coo, make baby sounds. The only occasions I wasn't spending my time with Dženana was when I went to school or when I hung out with my friends in the evening. As soon as I got together with my friends, I'd begin, "Hey, guys, you know what Dženana did today? She banged her head when I was listening to Metallica." Everyone would listen intently and laugh with me.

I didn't know if it was part of stress or something else, but my asthma that had developed during the war was turning for the worse. Every single morning at 5:00 a.m., I'd wake up wheezing and coughing. My chest felt as if it was being crushed by a ton of concrete, which made me lose all my body strength. I'd take a couple of puffs out of my inhaler, and I would continue to wheeze and cough for about an hour until it finally subsided and let me go back to sleep. Asthma made me tired, and I couldn't run even a few steps without having an asthma attack. One time, on my way home at the crack of dawn from Jasmina's, I heard a wheezing sound as I walked down the street. I'd turn around to check whether it was an animal that I recalled hearing when we went camping before the war. But every time I turned around, I saw nothing but inanimate objects in their usual places. It took me a while to realize it was the sound of my breathing. I hadn't listened to my breathing until that point, and I was taken by surprise that my body had become so fragile. I felt as if I was falling apart.

Yet, I continued to smoke. I was constantly surrounded by smoke all the time, so it made no difference if I smoked or not. But I felt I should do something about it. I should quit, but my smoking habit was so ingrained that I didn't know how. I realized it was time for me to take care of myself. War was over, better times were to come, and I sure needed to be ready for them.

CHAPTER 23

Returning Home

hen the rich wage war, it's the poor who die.
—Jean-Paul Sartre

IN DECEMBER, we heard our home in Aerodromsko Naselje was going to be recaptured from the Serbs by March 1996. I couldn't wait to walk on the familiar paths again. The day my neighborhood was liberated, I eagerly awaited the day of our return home. I couldn't visualize at the time what would be remaining upon arrival in my neighborhood, but I hoped I would at least find my childhood photographs. I wondered if I would see again the bed on which I had slept, the desk on which I wrote my homework, or anything that would bring me back to any reminders of my past.

The day I approached the entrance of Aerodromsko Naselje, for the first time in four years, tears came to my eyes. In front of me lay a deserted wasteland. The buildings, destroyed by many shells, looked as if they were oft hit by a wrecking ball. One whole side of a building lay on the ground, flattened to its foundation. On some buildings, the walls were pierced with dozens of shells, and I could clearly see through the building, looking at another wreck across the street. The little kiosk where I used to buy candies as a child looked like an old metal box, corroded from exposure to the rain. The bakery—next to the deserted and wet supermarket—was flat and without walls. I couldn't see a roof on any building. With each step on the street, I encountered shell craters shaped like roses and anxious reminders of many who had been killed or wounded. I crossed the park where boys once played soccer, and I saw my building, a ruin sitting on the street where the trees, roses, grass, and everything were overgrown. The buildings looked small to me. I thought, perhaps, I had grown up.

The cherry trees my father planted in the front and back had grown high to the heavens. I looked around the buildings to find evidence of the enemy massacre of our neighbors. Rains must have washed everything away, for I could see no bloody marks anywhere. I hesitated to face my home. I knew that misery was inside. I desperately wanted to know if I would find anything in my apartment— perhaps a childhood photograph, my schoolbooks, my poetry, or my drawings? The entrance door was missing, and I entered the apartment through the void. The hallway was dark, empty, and cold. The dresser was missing. The parquet on the floor was taken, uncovering the cold white cement. The entire house was empty. It was open and airy, and there was nothing inside. They took everything, and I mean everything. They took the furniture, dishes, kitchen cabinets, window frames and sills, toilet seat, bathtub. Everything. It then occurred to me that the car my parents bought the year before the war was not in our garage. It was a brand-new Škoda that my parents were supposed to have paid for with writing sixty monthly checks the day they picked it up at the dealership. The smell of the new car was still present when my parents left home.

As I witnessed the emptiness, I wondered who had sat on our furniture, who had watched our TV, who had eaten from our plates, and who had burned our photographs. As I entered the living room, I discovered a little pile of notebooks and audiocassettes left behind by the enemy. I crouched and nervously looked through the pile to see if anything precious or valuable remained. I found my diary from when I was twelve years old and stared at it for a long time. I knew it was just a notebook, but I wrote my past in there. My diary was the only precious item I had found. I flipped through pages and felt as if I had never left home. But then, I looked around; the emptiness reminded me of the consequences of the war. I flipped to the last page and read: *I wish my diary lived forever! '89.*

I gazed at the corner of the room and remembered my mother sitting on our brown sectional with a needle in one hand and a thread wrapped around her pointer finger, creating a beautiful piece of crochet. Folk music played in the background, drawing out the sound of the pressure cooker in the kitchen. The needle in her hand would move so fast that my eyes couldn't grab a hold of it. She was the crochet master. The speed at which she created her art always amazed me. I wondered, How does she ever know what she is doing? She would place the crochet on the armrest of the sectional and gently cross over the surface with her hand. The smile on her face revealed satisfaction.

She would sigh deeply and ask me with a pleasant voice that often reminded me of the murmur of a green river, "Do you like it?"

"Yes, Mom, you're the master of making crochet! You have golden hands I caressed many times to be healed from the chemicals you use cleaning the house. Please, Mom, don't expose your tender hands to these chemicals... I want you to make these crochets forever. And when I get married and buy a house, I want to have them around to remind me of your beautiful, hardworking hands."

I returned from the past again and realized my dreams would be unfulfilled. The crochets my mother had made were burned or stolen with every other physical piece of my past. We found nothing valuable in the house—it was empty like a shell without its pearl.

I went out on the balcony to view the building across from ours. It was hollow but full of the memories of those who innocently died there. Our neighbor Husnija—a bus driver before the war who lived on the first floor across from our building, with his wife, two children, and his mother—was killed the morning the enemy occupied the neighborhood. His mother stood next to him, perhaps with deep sadness yet relief she was about to leave the world, for she couldn't stand the pain of her son's death. I could hear silence filled with the enemy's shouting: "Get out of the buildings right now!" And I could see the people either run in fear or give in to the enemy. For sure, they couldn't escape this evil force. I looked around, trying to remember my neighbors, their faces, and interactions with them, and it seemed to me the past I tried to recall was buried in the ground with deep roots of home security, happiness, and satisfaction.

I closed my eyes for a second and clenched my teeth. The image I had in my mind was disturbing, painful. For I knew the scenes were real. Leaning on the wall and waiting to be executed, some of my neighbors looked at the enemy's hands, waiting for the finger to pull the trigger. That enemy's finger had no connection to a healthy mind as it was focused on its own devilish business. The finger would come closer and closer until the click sound became real. The neighbor would fall to his knees to the ground, dragging his body with them, and placing his bloody hands on the hot pavement. The last "Ahhhhh-hhh," followed by the enemy's uproarious laughter, and then the finger would move faster and faster, and neighbor after neighbor would fall like a deck of cards. The Serbian soldiers with beards and the *kokarda* on their hats approached the people lying on the ground, kicked their sides to uncover the hands, took off their jewelry, and walked away as if nothing had happened...

I opened my eyes to see if I had been dreaming, but that unusual scene of destruction suggested reality—reality for which I longed to change when, in fact, nothing was changeable.

I went to my room, looked through my glassless window, and saw the airport, which seemed useless. The elm trees lined by the main street looked even higher, but they were gray, sad, and dull. Children would no longer play between the trees, because the land was now potentially full of mines. The main street between my home and the airport was empty. The sound of planes—history.

169

I came out of the apartment free from anticipation, but not sorrow and despair. The hedges on the little pathway leading to the street were high since they remained untended for years. With a deep gaze into the leafless hedge, I noticed the colors. I approached them and realized there was a photograph in the hedges. It was a photograph of my young mother sitting on a fence with sunglasses, smiling.

I yelled, "Mama, look what I found!"

Everyone gathered to see the miracle of the one photo that had survived. I returned looking around, hoping I would find my favorite photograph of Amra and me standing next to each other in the kindergarten. My father used to carry that photograph to show his colleagues his cute little daughters.

But after searching, I saw nothing but the dirty little patches of snow on the ground.

CHAPTER 24

❧

Sarajevo Reintegration

ut when will our leaders learn—war is not the answer.
—Helen Thomas

AFTER THE AERODROMSKO NASELJE REINTEGRATION, Grbavica and Ilidža, and all other parts of Sarajevo occupied by Serbs during the war, were returned to the Bosnians. When I woke up the following morning, Jasmina called me to let me know she had heard from Zlatan that Ogi disappeared. He vanished and was nowhere to be found. We gathered at Zlatan's place the same night, like detectives trying to solve a mystery. The three of us sat in a smoky room, speculating over where he might have gone. Zlatan was hungover, and had enormous circles around his gigantic eyes.

"I don't know. I'm not smart enough to know."

"Zlatan, tell me. Please tell me. You were the last one to see him. What did he tell you?" Jasmina pleaded.

"He said nothing. He seemed pretty normal. Everything was cool."

Zlatan and Jasmina speculated that he might have been kidnapped, but it was difficult to guess by whom exactly. Perhaps the aftermath of the war already brought chaos, and people were already lining up for revenge upon others for their evil deeds. Was Ogi in real trouble? Did he owe anything to anybody? What could have happened to him? We hoped that he would be found soon, alive. They kept speculating, as that was the only thing they could do with the absence of any type of information.

I said nothing. Nothing crossed my mind about why he left. There could have been a million different reasons he had disappeared. To where, I couldn't even begin.

Jasmina's mourning began when, day after day, Ogi was nowhere to be found. She'd call his mother every day in the beginning to find out if he called, sent a letter, or gave a sign of life. When the answer continued to be negative, she called every other day. Every other day turned into occasionally, until the phone calls ceased completely. She had to accept his disappearance.

I consoled her as much as I could, though, being dumbfounded by his disappearance, my only form of support was to be there for her, physically.

Finally, the day arrived when Jasmina's phone rang, and it was Ogi's mother on the other end of the line. She had heard from Ogi.

"Where is he?" Jasmina was anxious and relieved at the same time that the news had arrived.

"He is in Republika Srpska."

Apparently, when the city reintegration took place, people could walk to the Republika Srpska freely. Being shot while crossing the border was now a thing of the past. Ogi, one early morning around six, headed toward Grbavica and, like he was being pulled by a strange force, kept on walking until he landed on the other side. These lands were inaccessible to us during the war. We didn't know how safe it was to venture to the other side now that the war was over. The people who lived there might have been the same people who were shooting at us, and even if it was safe, the question was whether we were ready to face them.

Ogi left to find his old love. When the war broke out, she went to the Serbian side, and all connections between her and Ogi were cut off. Later, we found out that, upon finding her, he decided not to return so he could be with her. Eventually, they ended up marrying and having a child.

When Jasmina found out about Ogi finding his ex and deciding to stay with her, she took it hard. While the good news was that he was still alive, the bad news was that he was now in another woman's arms. She talked about it nonstop. "Why did he leave me? I thought we loved each other. He told me he did. How dare he up and go just like that and not tell me? Is it something I did to make him take off?"

Zlatan and I listened, day in and day out, but we couldn't do or say much to console her. Her loss was deep. It seemed as if someone had cut her right arm off. She no longer had an interest in doing anything fun. Unexpectedly, I had not seen her for a few days. I discovered that she was taken to the emergency room. Jasmina tried to end her own life by poisoning herself with pills. When her brother discovered her in her room, he took her to the ER immediately, where they pumped her stomach. I came to visit her the following day, and she looked white as a ghost and completely lifeless.

It took several weeks for Jasmina to recover from this experience. While not completely recovered, she could function normally, cut her losses, and continued on with her life, accepting that even though the war was over, everything continued to be fragile and short-lived.

Returning to our previous fashion, Jasmina and I continued to rummage through the city and meet different people, which seemed like a perfect distraction from her pain. In the spring, we met three brothers who used to live in Dobrinja but were forced to leave mainly like the rest of us. Their old apartment in Dobrinja was quite large—three bedrooms, with a piano sitting in the foyer. During the war, they lived in Grbavica where, we soon found out, the Serbian Army put them in charge to fulfill their logistical needs. From what they told us, they now lived in a one-bedroom apartment, all five of them, and could barely make ends meet.

The three brothers were musicians. Robert, the oldest, played bass guitar while the middle brother, Gordan, was a drummer. And the youngest, Vedran, was a guitar player. They had access to a garage that served as a studio, so Jasmina and I visited them frequently to listen to them play music. We picked up the instruments and mess around. For war survivors who had gone through many life challenges, the brothers were always laughing and had a great attitude all the time. Shortly after, we became inseparable and spent most of our free time together. Vedran and I dated, and while he, like the others, remained unsuccessful in trying to kiss me, he had not given up on me. I liked him. I liked his long hair and the way he talked. He was a superb listener, and he wanted to make me happy. Meanwhile, Jasmina and Robert began dating, so we often went out on double dates, some-times with Gordan being a third wheel, but still welcomed company.

My asthma was getting worse day by day. I couldn't breathe at all, day or night, and there was not much I could have done about it for the lack of right intervention or medicine. One day, we gathered near the Miljacka River in Grbavica, and we all took a smoke. I coughed violently while they all helplessly watched me. When I finally came to my senses, I flicked the cigarette up in the air, tossing it as far as I could.

"That is it! I quit." That was the end of my smoking. I quit cold turkey. Vedran was quite supportive, and whenever I felt the urge to take a cigarette out of a pack and light it, he would gently remind me why I had quit. But those urges didn't come often, as I knew what affects they had on me and how painful the asthma attacks could be.

A few months had passed when my relationship with Vedran blos-somed. On one occasion, Vedran said, jokingly or not, that I might be the one. A few days later, we planned on getting together and met at the bridge in Grbavica, a few blocks from his home. I arrived there right on time. Punctuality always mattered to me, and I expected the same in return when making plans with friends. Vedran was not there when I arrived, so I waited.

Ten minutes had already passed, and Vedran was still not showing up. Since we had no cell phones to communicate tardiness, the assumption was always that plans were still on unless over fifteen minutes had passed.

Out of nowhere, a skinny man who might have been in his forties and looked like a bum came up to me and said, "Wanna give me a blow job for twenty marks?" I looked at him in disbelief about what I had just heard. "Wanna give me a blow job for twenty marks?" he repeated one more time, and when I was certain about what he had said, I walked as far away from him as I could. When Vedran finally arrived, I was livid. He apologized for being late, but I did not want to hear it or his reasons.

I looked at him, with anger written all over my face, and finally said, "We are through!" I turned around and walked away. That was the end of my relationship with Vedran.

The war aftermath brought yet more strange times.

CHAPTER 25

Marching Forward

$\mathcal{W}$ar would end if the dead could return.
—Stanley Baldwin

MAY 1996 couldn't come soon enough. I was about to graduate from high school. My classmate Lejla, a beautiful girl with long blond hair, was injured in her karate class. She had broken a bone in her leg that was never properly attended to. Eventually, she was diagnosed with bone cancer. Two months later, she died. It was time for mourning, but I didn't know what to do with this information. My mind couldn't grasp that someone could die of a natural death. How could someone survive the war, a hero surviving the unimaginable, and then die of cancer? My mother cried when she heard this. She was fighting her own postwar demons, and she was easily triggered. When she reflected on my high school days and how my teenage years had passed, directionless and futureless, she would cry even more. There was something about being a helpless parent, forced to turn into a surviving body and hoping your children would remain intact.

I'd try to see the positives from coming out of the war and facing life's new possibilities and prospects. I would prepare for college, and I was happy that my trips downtown to attend lectures would become more meaningful. To graduate from high school, I had to defend my thesis, a subject of my own choosing. I chose biology. Since Amra was pregnant, I explored fetus growth. Our school had gained personal computers, but I was too timid to use one, as I had never seen a personal computer before. I was afraid I would break it or do something that would cause irreparable damage. So I used a typewriter that my father had borrowed from work. I had to defend my thesis in front of three high school teachers, one of whom was my biology teacher. She had the reputation of being stern and demanding with students, but I always thought her lectures made sense, and her presentation style always grabbed me.

The thesis defense took place in a cramped classroom. I felt confident about my thesis defense because I could visualize everything I had discovered about fetus growth—all the different growth stages. I would picture my little niece growing, who was already born with her tiny nose, red lips, blond hair, and beautifully rounded cheeks. My biology teacher asked me one question, to which I responded without hesitation. I passed my thesis with a B+ grade, and I concluded that chapter of my life. I was ready to move onto the next stage—going to college and gaining an education that would give me future prospects.

It took me several months to figure out what I wanted to study. After some consideration, I decided to study pharmacy, a field that was remotely related to my thesis, but close enough to steer me in one direction. My affinity for chemistry was lacking since primary school, but Anis helped me prepare for the entrance exam for the pharmacy college. When I took the exam, I wasn't sure about the answer to one of the exam questions, so I peeked at the sheet of a person sitting below me and I put down the same answer whether the answer was right or wrong. That year, the pharmacy college was only accepting sixty applicants, and on the day of the entrance exam, I saw at least a hundred students, like me, hoping to be accepted. Without personal connections, my chances of getting in were pretty slim since my talent for natural sciences wasn't quite up to par.

My mother knew someone who knew someone who was in the pharmacy school. She promptly contacted those people and pleaded for me to get in. When the results were released, I went to the college to find out if I had been accepted. If I didn't score high enough on the exam, I was still guaranteed entrance, so I wasn't too concerned. When I arrived at the school, I found the sheets of paper taped to the door with all the applicants' names. Right below the sixtieth name was a line separating the accepted students from the rejected. I found my name in the fifty-ninth place, which meant I was accepted without intervention by my mother. Things were looking up. Now that I was guaranteed a spot in college, I was relieved and continued to hang out downtown with Jasmina, getting drunk every night.

We'd hang out at a newly opened Internet café where I learned about e-mail and the Internet. For the first time, I learned how to send an e-mail with AOL. I didn't know how to open up an account of my own, so I relied on whoever was there and was willing to share their e-mail address. The only people I knew who had an e-mail address were the foreigners who had visited Sarajevo and left their contact information behind. Little did I know that their response would never reach me unless I saw the person who let me use their e-mail account again. For me, though, the Internet café wasn't necessarily a place to get in touch with foreigners. I went there to drink, ending up hanging out with random people who would eventually befriend us and buy us beers.

We met several people at the Internet café, most of whom were foreigners. There was Peter, an Australian, who wore a tie with kangaroo prints. He only stayed in Sarajevo for a few days, as he was en route to other parts of Europe. He was on an extensive trip and traveling all over the world. Then there were Jim and Jim, one from California and one from Chicago. There was also Mario, who was born in Croatia but lived in the United States. They all worked as peacekeepers in war-torn Bosnia and frequented at the café.

One evening, while sipping beers at the Internet café, the two Jims

—whom we later referred to as Chicago Jim and California Jim—devised a plan to give us a guided tour of the outskirts of Sarajevo in Republika Srpska. The war had just ended, but I was still frightened by the thought of running into Serb soldiers who'd wanted to rape or kill me, especially now that their war could be perceived as lost. Chicago Jim looked at us both in the eye and promised that we would be safe. He spoke as if he was our bodyguard and savior, and when I noticed his confidence and reassurance of how important he felt as our protector, the question came to mind: Where were you in 1992 to stop all the horrors? Being a savior was easy now.

I couldn't be too critical of Chicago Jim, because he seemed kind and good natured. To us Bosnians, he looked like a real American, as if he just came out of an action movie, with blonde hair, blue eyes, straight white teeth, and a muscular body. He'd wear dark wide sunglasses, as if he were blind, and Jasmina and I made fun of him by putting a hand palm over our eyes as to imitate his look.

The following day, we got together with the Jims to drive around in their big black Chevrolet. The car was two times the size of a Fiat, a tiny car my father used to drive before the war. When my parents upgraded to a Škoda the year before the war, we enjoyed the extra leg space, though since we only had it for a short while, we never got used to it being ours. It belonged to Serbs now. We all hopped in the Chevrolet, Jasmina and I in the back as if getting ready for a trip of a lifetime. Luckily, the windows were tinted, so even if we ran into Serbs, they wouldn't be able to see our faces covered in terror and fear. As we approached Republika Srpska, I felt my palms sweating and my heart beating like it was about to jump out of my chest. I reached for Jasmina's hand and I felt her sweat joining mine. I only hoped that Jims had a gun or two on them, so that if we got pulled over and attacked, they'd truly be able to protect us.

California Jim smelled our fear. He was louder than Chicago Jim and drank like a sailor. To ease the situation, he'd exclaim as loudly as possible, yelling out "Pale!", the place where many Sarajevo Serbs migrated to at the beginning of the war and the direction we were heading. He was driving fast and furious, and I felt as if he just bought the car and was showing it off. He yelled again "Pale!" causing Jasmina and I to let out a nervous laughter. We didn't get to Pale, but he drove us through the places that belonged to Serbs during the war and were eventually returned to the Bosnians. Much of that land had been planted with mines and everyone knew to avoid them. We finally stopped at Vrace near Mount Trebević, a place once occupied by Serb tanks to fire upon Sarajevo, the first piece of news our neighbor relayed to us in our basement at the beginning of the war.

The Jims jumped out of the Chevrolet and opened the back doors for us to follow them. Both Jasmina and I hesitated, as if for a second, we thought the Americans were playing us and were about to give us away for prosecution. They reassured us once again we were safe, and each gave his hand for comfort.

Vrace Park, where the view of Sarajevo was open and unob-structed, seemed as if a gang of hooligans had partied all night, trashing every cultural artifact they could find. This high ground was where Serb tanks, stolen from the Yugoslav Army, stood until only recently they had been displaced. This was the place where the Serbs would plot attacks on innocent civilians and fire mortars into the streets of Sarajevo. This was where Serbs daydreamed of penetrating the city and completely occupying Sarajevo. As I looked around, I thought to myself how meaningless the war had been. It couldn't have been a holy war justified by differences between two religions. My parents, or any other Muslims we knew, never mention the idea that Muslims wanted Bosnia for themselves. We were a peaceful people. No one had ever heard of such an idea until a Serbian politician invented it to invoke and justify the hate of peaceful neighbors. How could the Serbian people as a whole buy it? Were they just itching for an excuse to go to war? Or a reason to believe they were a superior?

Seeing all the trash made me angry, so I went back to the Chevrolet and waited for the rest of them. We eventually arrived back in Sarajevo, intact with all our pieces. Part of me felt that the "trip of the lifetime" was a terrible decision, as I knew my life was completely upside down and it would never be the same. I didn't have to have it rubbed in my face by seeing the scenes of vandalism and nonsensical destruction.

After the trip, we saw the Jims less and less. They either got deployed to other parts of Bosnia or they no longer wanted to witness the lost piece of youth that we sadly carried on our shoulders. Or perhaps something else. But we kept going to the Internet café and meeting new people.

Then there was a happy older fellow who befriended us one night. He got drunk and, while under the influence, requested "Killing Me Softly" to play. He sang along with the song and kept ordering beers for himself and us. That was the first and last time we saw him. There were the two English brothers. Their mother was Croatian, so they spoke and understood a little of Bosnian, but their pronunciation was often incorrect and comical to us. We met plenty of locals, but it was mostly foreigners we hung out with.

But none of that seemed fulfilling. My depression was sitting on my shoulders like a demon laughing at my weaknesses and my inability to snap out of it. Rage and depression, taking turns on duty, were dragging me down, and I didn't know what to do about it. They grew on me like a cancer, like something that you wanted to get rid of, but it kept growing at a rapid and uncontrollable rate. At home, I'd find refuge in music, listening while staring at the ceiling and absorbing the words of Bijelo Dugme's songs. When I wanted a change, I'd take an earring hoop and stab my ear until a new hole was made, and then again, and then again to make another one. In my numbness, I didn't feel pain. The war had made me tough, but peace now promised hope and a future. The war was behind me. It was time to move forward, despite the emptiness in my soul.

CHAPTER 26

High School Prom

$\mathcal{I}$f we don't end war, war will end us.
—H. G. Wells

MY HIGH SCHOOL organized a prom in a restaurant outside of Sarajevo, a place called Ilidža occupied by Serbs during the war. We were told to meet in front of the school where a bus would pick us up and drive us to the destination. My wardrobe was limited, so my mom suggested I wear Amra's wedding suit. I put some makeup on, made up my hair, and found my way to the school. My mom decided she would walk with me to send me off.

When we arrived, my classmates looked young and beautiful, all dressed up and ready to go. There were about thirty students in my class, split into two groups. A professional photographer took our pictures; we were standing in a classroom, attempting to smile and show pride for what we just accomplished. Graduating a high school during the war was no small task.

When we arrived at the restaurant, the buffet table awaited us with all kinds of food. How quickly was one to move onto good things, as if the war didn't even happen? Only a few months ago, we still had our food mixed in egg and milk powder. I looked at my classmates on the dance floor, smiling and dancing, clearly enjoying themselves. They strangely looked happy and centered. I realized not all of us experienced the war the same way. Some took it harder than others. But I was happy that they could move forward and carry on with joy so quickly, as if all that was behind us had been erased from memory.

I walked outside to find refuge from the loud music and catch some fresh air, as I wasn't able to breathe. Outside on my left was a building reduced to rubble, and on the other, a pile of trash and burnt cars. The remnants of the war couldn't be escaped just yet. I wondered how long it would take to clean up all the war-made mess. I looked up at the sky and clearly saw the Little and Big Dipper, a lesson learned in one of my geography classes. The summer triangle should be around somewhere as well. I sat down to observe and, at a particular moment, had a storm of memories from the recent past overcome me. I thought of its aftermath.

Because of the war, hundreds of thousands of people had lost their lives. Many children became orphans, many families lost their homes, and now were considered displaced. Many soldiers—men, young and old—died in battle or lost a limb or two from shrapnel. Many women were raped by the enemy, delivering unwanted babies made from pure evil. Many people simply went crazy as they couldn't bear the circumstances of the war. Many families were split into pieces, mothers losing all their children, sometimes on the same day. That was war. And for what? For someone's irrational ideals? For someone's own self-interest? All at the expense of the innocent?

And what about our identity? Now that Yugoslavia no longer existed, our newly formed country, Bosnia and Herzegovina, would need to find its own voice. The street names would soon be replaced by newly fallen heroes and politicians, and the war voices would echo for a long time. It was time to rebuild and make the country strong and proud. What about my identity? Who did I become? What kind of person did the war make me into? What would have I become under normal circumstances? Who could we trust from here on, and who were our loyal friends? Who was by our side during the war, and who was there only to profiteer from the chaos?

The moon was moving across the sky quickly, the music from the restaurant was traveling through the air, and the laugher of my classmates was making me nostalgic.

And then I contemplated my own experiences. My family and I lost our home. Uncle Ramiz died, but all of us in my nuclear family were still alive, all in one piece. If life was worth anything, we were fortunate enough to still have it. How was it we survived? I thought it must have been thousands of invisible beautiful angels singing prayers loudly against the sound of over ten thousand shells, among a half million I had heard fall on the streets of Sarajevo during the war. It was a miracle of sorts—a lucky star hanging above us. As I looked up at the sky, I felt a piece of the universe looking vast and beautiful in newfound peace. I was feeling hope as the sound of music and laugher traveled to my ears.

***

If you enjoyed this book at all, please leave a review even if it's only a sentence. Thank you!

Amra pretending to play the guitar, circa 1993.

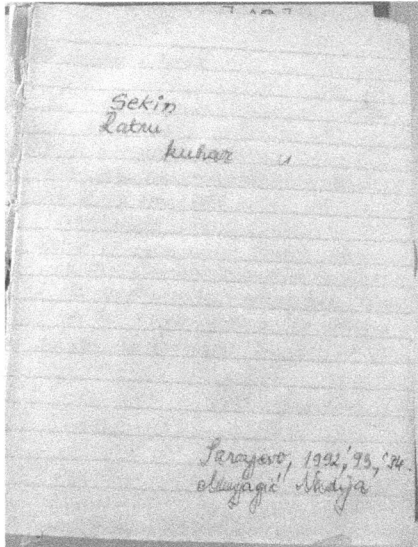

War recipe notebook

War recipe for Nutella, "almost like real"

Enisa, myself, and Selma hanging out at the back of my building in Dobrinja Five, circa 1994

Dado, myself, and Jasmina at an old-night party

High school circa 1995

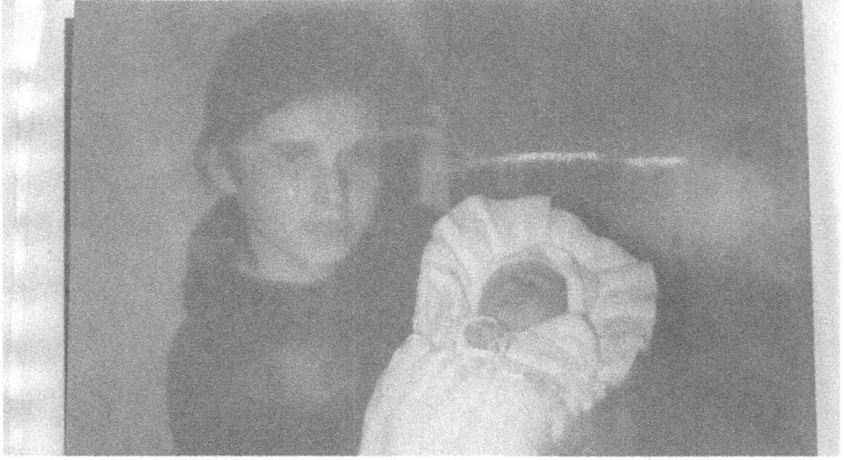

Dzenana and I, the day Dzenana was born

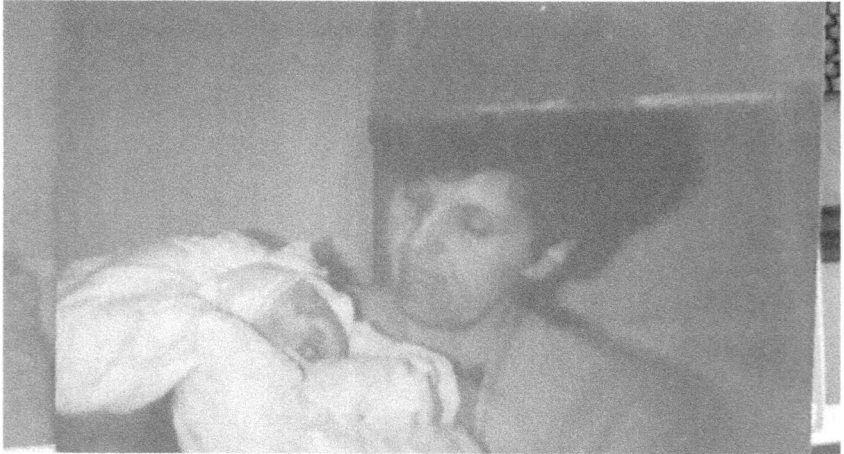

Dzenana and my mother, the day Dzenana was born

Among ruins, shortly after the war ended

Jasmina upon return home, circa 1996

Jasmina upon return home, 1996

Dzenana and I in our Dobrinja Five living room

ABOUT BOSNIA AND
HERCEGOVINA

About Bosnia and Herzegovina[1]

Bosnia and Herzegovina is a country with rich background and history. It has claimed its independence numerous times, with different country borders throughout history, but it has always been subject to occupation by others. The history is so complicated that, for the same reason, I choose not to go into great detail. Pertinent to this memoir, however, you will need to understand the basics and who the major players during the war were.

When the Austro-Hungarian power was overthrown with the beginning of World War I, a Yugoslav kingdom was built, first starting with the countries of Slovenia and Croatia and slowly building to what became the Social Federal Republic Yugoslavia with Josip Broz Tito as president. Yugoslavia consisted of six republics—Slovenia, Croatia, Bosnia and Herzegovina, Serbia, Monte Negro, and Macedonia (from west to east) and two autonomous republics, Vojvodina and Kosovo, adjacent to Serbia. The main language spoken in Yugoslavia was called Serbo-Croatian, even though each republic had its own dialects and variations of the language. Slovenia and Macedonia had their own language, which was distinctly different from Serbo-Croatian. Both Latin and Cyrillic alphabets were used.

The main religions in the former Yugoslavia were Orthodox Christianity, Catholicism, and Islam. People known as today's Bosnians emigrated from the north in the second century. It was Slavs that therefore gave the name to the country (Yugo, meaning south and Slavia, the origin). In the fifteenth century, the church separated Catholicism on the west and Orthodox on the east. In the land where Croatia now sits, people are predominantly Christian Catholics, and in Serbia, they are predominantly Christian Orthodox. With Bosnia and Herzegovina sitting in the middle, the population was mixed.

In the fifteenth century, the Ottoman Empire took over the land and ruled for nearly four centuries. During their occupation in Bosnia, they left cultural marks, including the architecture, the language, and some customs. When they ruled the country, they offered the incentive for people to convert to Islam by not having them pay their property taxes.

For the most part, Yugoslavia was secular, and the communist party prohibited its members to openly follow their religious beliefs. This was more so the case for Muslims. Because the Muslims in the country lacked their national identity, unlike their Bosnian Christian counterparts, population in Bosnia was simply identified as Serbs for Christian Orthodox, Croats for Christian Catholics, and Muslims. Despite the lack of identity, the most dominant religion in Bosnia and Herzegovina was Islam, with its population of around 45 percent before the 1992–1995 war.

When Tito died in 1980, political unrest began to brew in the country. The politicians couldn't agree on directions of the country that each republic had visualized. The tension grew to the point where Slovenia finally decided to part from Yugoslavia. Serbia wanted to keep the whole country intact, and head of the Socialist Party of Serbia at the time, Slobodan Milošević, set ultimatums that no politician could agree to. Then followed the independence of Croatia, and war began in the country shortly after.

Bosnia and Herzegovina had three major political parties, each representing a major religion. The head of the Muslim political party was Alija Izetbegović, who became the chief person in war affairs and negotiations. The head of the Serbian political party was Radovan Karadžić, who was getting orders from Serbia, mainly Slobodan Milošević. And the head of the Croatian party was Stjepan Kljuić. In short, when Bosnia and Herzegovina announced it would claim independence in 1992, Serbia had accused Bosnian Muslim politicians that they had wanted to build a homogeneous country with only Muslims living there. They had placed fear in Serbs that all of them would eventually be sent to Serbia. In order to prevent the Bosnian Muslims from doing so, they had begun tactics of brain-washing Serbs and building the propaganda that would turn Serbs against Muslims. Radovan Karadžić threatened Bosnian Muslims to drive them to extinction.

Bosnia and Herzegovina claimed its independence on March 1, 1992. Shortly after, a war broke out in the country. The Serbs had taken over most of the former Yugoslav military power and artillery. The war was mainly against Muslims, but it is important to note that many Serbs did not fall for the Serbian propaganda and fought along their Muslim and Croat neighbors. As a result of the war, hundreds of thousands of civilians had lost their lives. The war was considered one of the most brutal wars in the Balkans of all times. Ultimately, the war was about the attempt to gain personal power and wealth of a number of certain politicians.

The war was concluded in December 1995 with the Dayton Agreement signed in Paris. NATO had previously bombed positions occupied by Serbs and disabled their operations to continue with military attacks. The Dayton Agreement had separated the country into two distinct regions: Federal Republic, 51 percent of the land that mainly belonged to Muslims and Croats, and Republika Srpska, belonging to Bosnian Serbs. To this day, this divide still causes political and economic instability in the country. Some Serbs still deny the atrocities done to the Bosnian Muslims, so I imagine this book would not fare well in their eyes.

NOTES

ABOUT BOSNIA AND HERCEGOVINA

1. I am by no means an expert in the Bosnian history. The information provided here is derived primarily from my knowledge and memories. For more detailed information about Bosnian history, I recommend Bosnia: A Short History by Noel Malcolm

ACKNOWLEDGMENTS

The process of writing and editing the manuscript has not been easy at times, not only because English as a second language still represents some challenges for me but also because writing about the war felt like reliving it all over again. It seemed like a living nightmare at times. As I wrote the details, I realized what a troubled teenager I was, the state that might have amplified upon my arrival in the United States, given that now I had to contend with leaving my family, adapting to the new and different culture, and living in an abusive marriage.

I want to thank all my friends for being forgiving toward me for all my potential shortcomings and never giving up on me: Carolina, Viviana, Ivan, Kelly, Michelle, Christian, Eileen, Jennifer, Thomas, Sean, and Frank, who is smiling at us from the heaven above. You were my rock when the ground beneath me felt like shaky sand. It appeared as if you knew me better than I knew myself.

I want to thank my friend Ivan Schneider, who read the few first chapters and sparked the idea for the book title. I also want to thank my family in Sarajevo, especially my mother, who helped revive many of the stories written in the book. While they kept saying they didn't want to be reminded of the horrors, they generously offered a few details here and there that were crucial in describing some of the stories. I want to thank my beloved sister, Amra, who sent me the few war photos we had taken during the war.

Last but not the least, this book would not have been possible had it not been for my husband, Chad, who gave me much support during the writing process. If it wasn't for his words of encouragement, the manuscript would still be collecting dust.

He gave me much strength, his generous time to edit the manuscript, as well as needed hugs when the wounds felt fresh all over again. I am forever indebted and grateful for his love.

I am thankful for the experience of writing itself as it ultimately brought on healing and peace.

LET'S KEEP IN TOUCH!

I love to hear from my readers and also share news on my new releases, free content and book promos! For updates, please make sure to subscribe on Nadija Mujagic - Author Website

As a thank you for being a valuable reader, please grab a free copy of my short story *Under Walnuts*, mentioned in *Immigrated*:

Under Walnuts: A Short Story

ALSO BY NADIJA MUJAGIC

TILL A
BETTER WORLD

A NOVEL

Nadija Mujagic

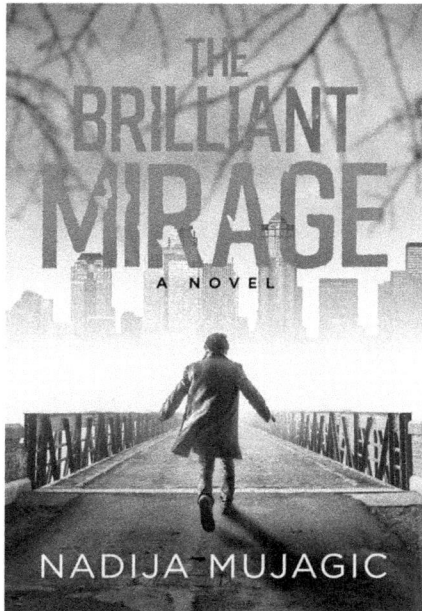

THE BRILLIANT MIRAGE

A NOVEL

NADIJA MUJAGIC

NADIJA MUJAGIC

THE EXCHANGE

A NOVEL

ABOUT THE AUTHOR

Nadija Mujagić was born and raised in Sarajevo, Bosnia and Herzegovina, what used to be the former Yugoslavia back in the late 1970s. In 1997, she moved to the United States shortly after the end of the Bosnian War and has lived in Massachusetts since. In her spare time, she enjoys playing sports and electric bass guitar.

To subscribe for news on new releases, visit Nadija Mujagic - Author page

www.ingramcontent.com/pod-product-compliance
Lightning Source LLC
Chambersburg PA
CBHW070926030426
42336CB00014BA/2555